Illinois Legal Research

Illinois Legal Research

Mark E. Wojcik
Associate Professor of Law
The John Marshall Law School

CAROLINA ACADEMIC PRESS
Durham, North Carolina

Copyright © 2003
Mark E. Wojcik
All Rights Reserved.

ISBN 0-89089-339-X
LCCN 2003110318

CAROLINA ACADEMIC PRESS
700 Kent Street
Durham, North Carolina 27701
Telephone (919) 489-7486
Fax (919) 493-5668
www.cap-press.com

Printed in the United States of America

To my students—past, present, and future.

The profession of the Law, when clothed in its true dignity and purity and strength, must rank first among the callings of men. Law rules the universe; "her seat is the bosom of God; her voice is the harmony of the world; all things in heaven and earth do her homage, the very least as feeling her care, and the greatest as not exempt from her power." What comprehensiveness! If to law herself may be applied such language, what may be said of that profession whose work is to formulate, to harmonize, to regulate, to adjust, to administer those rules and principles that underlie and permeate all government and society, and control the varied reactions of man? As thus viewed, there attaches to the legal profession a nobleness that cannot but be reflected in the life of the true lawyer, who, conscious of its greatness, and honest in the pursuit of his purpose, embraces the richness of learning, the profoundness of wisdom, the firmness of integrity and the purity of morals, together with the graces of modesty, courtesy and the general amenities of life.

To attain the highest excellence, the lawyer must possess the most varied and opposite qualities, and know how and when to use them; with depth and firmness of understanding, they must combine the keenness of acute discernment; learned in the subtleties of legal lore, let him at the same time know men, have tact to deal with them, and be rich in the enlarged beauties of classical learning; besides being a student, he must be able to leave the solitude of the study and adapt himself to the practical and every-day doings of men. It is his to command the respect of superiors, and again appeal to the weaknesses and infirmities of those less favored than himself; in fine, he must be "all things to all men."

Introduction, *The Bench and Bar of Chicago* 3 (American Biographical Publg. Co. 1904).

Contents

Foreword by Chief Justice Mary Ann G. McMorrow	xv
Preface and Acknowledgments	xvii

Chapter 1 Starting Out 3
  I. Introduction 3
  II. Some Differences between Research for Legal Writing Classes and Research for Real Clients 4
  III. Starting Your Research 5
    A. Determine the Parameters of the Assignment 5
    B. Create a List of Research Terms 8
    C. Create a List of Research Sources 10
  IV. The Most Overlooked Research Resource in the Law Library 12
  V. Ethical Duties of Legal Research 13
  VI. Getting Off of the Research Wheel 14
  VII. Chapter Summary 14
  Additional Resources 15

Chapter 2 The Illinois Constitution 17
  I. Introduction 17
  II. Illinois before Statehood 19
    A. First Peoples 19
    B. French Claims 20
    C. English Claims 21
    D. Illinois as Part of Virginia 22
    E. The Northwest Ordinance of 1787 23
    F. The Territory of Illinois (1809) 24
  III. Illinois as a State 24
    A. The First Illinois Constitution (1818) 24
    B. The Second Illinois Constitution (1848) 29
    C. The Third Illinois Constitution (1870) 30

D. The Current Illinois Constitution (1970)	31
E. Special Rules for Citing the Illinois Constitution	33
IV. Chapter Summary	35
Additional Resources	35

Chapter 3 Illinois Judicial Decisions 37
I. Introduction	37
II. Overview of the Illinois State Court System	38
A. Illinois Supreme Court	38
1. Stare Decisis	38
2. Information about the Illinois Supreme Court	40
3. Illinois Supreme Court Opinions	41
4. How to Read a Citation	42
5. Finding Parallel Citations	43
B. Illinois Appellate Court	44
1. Finding Published Decisions	45
2. Illinois Appellate Court Decisions before 1935 Are Not Binding	46
3. "Unpublished" Decisions and Rule 23	46
C. Circuit Courts	48
1. Overview	48
2. Finding Information on the Circuit Courts	49
3. Appeals from the Circuit Court	50
4. Researching Circuit Court Decisions	51
5. Researching Civil Jury Verdicts and Settlements	52
6. Illinois Criminal Justice Information Authority	55
III. Illinois Court of Claims	56
IV. Federal Courts in Illinois	59
A. Overview	59
B. Interplay between the State and Federal Courts	59
1. Federal Question Jurisdiction and Pendent Jurisdiction	59
2. Pendent Jurisdiction	60
3. Removal	60
4. Diversity Jurisdiction	60

5. Two Views on Applying State Law	61
6. State Courts and Federal Precedent	62
V. A Few More Words about Case Reporters	63
A. Slip Opinions	63
B. Advance Sheets	63
C. Electronic Sources: Cases and Summaries	63
VI. Illinois Digests	65
A. Need for Digests	65
B. Headnotes	66
C. Never Quote a Headnote	66
D. Organization of the Digest	67
E. Use the Topic and Key Number from an Illinois Case to Find Other Illinois Cases	69
F. Use the Topic and Key Number from a Non-Illinois Case to Find an Illinois Case	69
G. The Wojcik Secret for Using the Illinois Digest – Five Up, Five Down	70
H. Finding a Topic and Key Number to Use in West's Illinois Digest	70
I. Updating Your Digest Research	71
VII. An Overlooked Research Resource: The Official Index	72
VIII. Sullivan's Judicial Profiles	73
IX. Summary	74
Additional Resources	74
Chapter 4 Illinois Statutes and Local Ordinances	77
I. Overview	77
II. Illinois Statutes	78
A. Session Laws	78
B. Illinois Compiled Statutes	78
C. Finding a Statute	80
D. Spell Check Warning	81
III. Interpreting Statutes	81
A. The Debate Over Using Legislative History	82
B. Finding Legislative History	86
1. Check the Annotated Statutes	86
2. Identify the Public Act Number	87

3. Find the Bill Number		87
4. Find the Indexes to Debates		87
5. Finding the Debates		88
6. House and Senate Journals		89
IV. Tracking Current Illinois Legislation		90
V. Citing Statutes from Other Jurisdictions		92
VI. Local Ordinances		93
Additional Resources		94

Chapter 5   Illinois Administrative Law   95
  I. Executive Branch   95
     A. State Constitutional Offices   95
     B. Illinois Attorney General   95
  II. Administrative Agencies   97
  III. How to Research Administrative Law   100
     A. Finding the Enabling Statute   101
     B. Finding Cases that Interpret the Enabling Statute   103
     C. Finding Illinois Regulations   104
     D. Finding Cases that Interpret the Regulations   105
     E. Finding Secondary Sources that Interpret the
        Statute or Regulations   106
  IV. Illinois Administrative Law Materials   106
     A. CD Rom, Websites, and Books   106
     B. Illinois Register   107
     C. Historical Research   107
     D. Decisions of Administrative Agencies   108
  Additional Resources   108

Chapter 6   Updating Primary Authority   111
  I. Why Update Authorities, and What Can Happen
     If You Don't?   111
  II. Using Shepard's Citators   114
     A. Using Shepard's in Print to Shepardize Cases   115
        1. Select the Shepard's   115
        2. "What Your Library Should Contain"   116
        3. Get to Work   116

Contents • xi

  4. Tips for Using Shepard's Effectively 117
  5. Daily Update Desk for Shepard's Citations 118
 B. Shepardizing Statutes and Regulations 119
 C. Shepardizing Other Primary Authorities 119
 D. Shepardizing Secondary Authority 120
III. KeyCite 120
IV. Leave to Appeal Table of Cases 121
V. Call the Court Clerk 121
VI. Using Sources as Search Terms 122
VII. Using Digests to Update Legal Rules 122
VIII. Chapter Summary 123
Additional Resources 123

Chapter 7 Secondary Sources 125
I. Introduction 125
 A. Secondary Sources as a Roadmap 125
 B. Using Secondary Sources to Start and
   Finish Research 126
 C. Choosing a Secondary Source: Learn about
   Your Tools 127
 D. Updating Secondary Sources 128
II. Legal Encyclopedias 129
 A. Three Functions of Legal Encyclopedias 129
 B. State Legal Encyclopedias for Illinois Law 131
 C. How to Use the Encyclopedias 133
 D. Citing Encyclopedias as Sources of Authority 134
III. Treatises 134
 A. Overview 134
 B. Finding a Treatise 135
 C. Using a Treatise 136
 D. When Should You Cite a Treatise? 137
IV. Law Review Articles 138
 A. Understanding Legal Periodicals 138
 B. Finding Law Review Articles and
   Bar Association Journals 139
 C. Citing Law Review Articles as Authority 143

V. Continuing Legal Education Materials	143
VI. Other Secondary Law Sources	144
A. Dictionaries	145
B. Restatements (Annotated)	145
C. Uniform Laws (Annotated)	146
D. A.L.R. Annotations	146
VII. Chapter Summary	147
Additional Resources	147
Chapter 8 Rules of Court and Rules of Ethics	**149**
I. Introduction	149
II. Researching Illinois Court Rules	150
A. Finding the Text of Court Rules	150
B. Finding Judicial Interpretations of the Court Rules	151
C. Finding Commentary on the Court Rules	152
III. Rules of Ethics	153
A. Ethical Rules for Judges	153
1. Substantive Rules	153
2. Illinois Courts Commission	153
B. Ethical Rules for Attorneys	153
1. Substantive Rules	153
2. Illinois Attorney Registration and Disciplinary Commission	154
C. Bar Association Ethics Opinions	155
IV. Updating Ethical Rules	156
V. Researching Local Federal Rules	156
Additional Resources	157
Chapter 9 Form Books, Forms, and Jury Instructions	**159**
I. Introduction	159
II. How to Use Form Books	161
A. Research First	161
B. Take Care When Combining Provisions	161
III. Finding Illinois Form Books	162
IV. Legal Forms from Cyberspace	164
V. Federal Court Forms	164

Contents • xiii

VI. Illinois Jury Instructions	165
Additional Resources	166
Chapter 10 Looseleaf Services	169
I. Introduction	169
II. Finding Looseleaf Services	171
III. Using Looseleaf Services in Print	172
IV. Citing Looseleaf Services	172
V. Using Computerized Databases as Looseleaf Services	173
Additional Resources	174
Chapter 11 Legal Citation	177
I. Six Citation Functions	177
A. Establish Authority	177
B. Minimize Distraction	177
C. Ensure Accuracy	178
D. Avoid Plagiarism	178
E. Promote Concise Writing	180
F. Show Subsequent Legal History	181
II. Citation Manuals	181
A. The Bluebook	181
B. The University of Chicago Maroon Book	183
C. The ALWD Citation Manual	183
D. Illinois Citation Rules	184
III. Samples of Specific Citations	185
Sample Citations	186
Additional Resources	193
Chapter 12 Electronic Legal Research	195
Additional Resources	197
Appendix A Website Addresses for Illinois Courts	201
Federal Courts	201
State Courts	202

Appendix B Selected Constitutional Offices, Administrative Agencies, and Special Government Commissions and Committees for the State of Illinois   205

Appendix C Illinois Legal Research Quiz   217

Index   221

Foreword

by Chief Justice Mary Ann G. McMorrow

The preamble to the Illinois Rules of Professional Conduct emphasizes that the "practice of law is a public trust." Lawyers are officers of the court vested with the responsibility of maintaining public confidence in our justice system by acting ethically and competently at all times. Pursuant to Rule 1.1 of the Illinois Rules of Professional Conduct, a lawyer is required to provide "competent representation" to a client. In turn, "competent representation" is defined by the Rule as having "the legal knowledge, skill, thoroughness and preparation necessary for the representation." A special task force of the American Bar Association on law schools and the legal profession authored a report that recognized that "[i]t can hardly be doubted that the ability to do legal research is one of the skills that any competent practitioner must possess."[1] That report concluded that "[i]n order to conduct legal research effectively, a lawyer should have a working knowledge of the nature of legal rules and legal institutions, the fundamental tools of legal research, and the process of devising and implementing a coherent and effective research design."[2]

Professor Wojcik's book provides a state-specific resource to aid both students and lawyers in researching Illinois case law, Illinois statues and local ordinances, Illinois administrative law, and other sources of legal information. Because of his many years of experience teaching courses in effective legal writing, Professor Wojcik has

---

1. Legal Education and Professional Development: An Educational Continuum, Report of the Task Force on Law Schools and the Profession: Narrowing the Gap 163 (1992).
2. Id.

had the opportunity to observe and identify the most problematic aspects of legal research. This book may assist both law students and law practitioners to overcome such problems.

Effective and persuasive legal advocacy is grounded in accurate and thorough legal research. A lawyer must be able to capably research the law to provide competent representation and to ensure that the high standards of the legal profession are upheld. This book outlines the fundamental principles of researching Illinois law, and should be a valuable addition to the libraries of Illinois lawyers.

Preface and Acknowledgments

For more than a decade, I have had the pleasure of teaching legal research and writing. Over these years, I have learned much about effective legal research tools and strategies. I am still learning, because there are so many developments in legal research materials and methods.

This book can be used in several ways:
1. New lawyers, law students, and paralegals who are familiar with (or who are now learning) research skills from national research texts can use this book as a state-specific supplement to the national legal research texts.
2. Law students and paralegals who are just beginning their studies can use this book as a primary tool for learning legal research skills in primary and secondary law sources. Armed with knowledge of one state's legal system and resources, a researcher can transpose that knowledge to other jurisdictions and to problems involving federal legal research.
3. Government employees, including those who work in the legislative, judicial, and executive branches of state government, can use this book for general guidance and specific tips on efficient legal research.
4. Political scientists, academics, members of the public, and librarians without specialized legal training can use this book as an introduction to legal research skills and resources available in Illinois.
5. Legal researchers in other jurisdictions can use this book to increase the efficiency of their research strategies for problems involving Illinois law.
6. New lawyers and experienced professionals can use this book to identify recent developments in legal research as

well as "legal research secrets" that will make all researchers more efficient and effective.

In preparing the materials for this book, I looked not only at Illinois legal materials, but also at research guides for other states. I found a marvelous book—*Florida Legal Research* written by Suzanne Rowe, Barbara Busharis, and Lisa Kuhlman Tietig. Carolina Academic Press published the first edition of that book in 1998, and the second edition in 2002.[1] The popularity and success of that book proved it to be a good general model for a state research guide – a book that was a teaching tool rather than a bibliographic compilation of state legal research sources. A book that would not necessarily replace the national research texts, but would explain the special sources of state legal research that are often ignored or only briefly mentioned.

This book on Illinois legal research thus owes much to Suzanne Rowe, Barbara Busharis, and Lisa Kuhlman Tietig. Although I had been working on various versions of *Illinois Legal Research* for several years before I found their book on Florida Legal Research, it was the format of their book that finally made this book a reality. It was also the success of that book that convinced Keith Sipe and Bob Conrow at Carolina Academic Press to allow me to prepare this first edition of *Illinois Legal Research* and to plan future volumes for other jurisdictions. These books are intended to become part of a national series of state-specific legal research guides to supplement national research texts.

Many judges, lawyers, law students, and law librarians from Illinois and across the country have helped me directly and indirectly with this present work. I am particularly grateful to Dorothy In-Lan Wang Li, Director of the Law Library at The John Marshall Law School, and to the professional law librarians and library staff who provided not only enthusiastic support and encouragement for this book, but also astute proofreading and editing assistance. This book

---

1. Barbara J. Busharis & Suzanne E. Rowe, *Florida Legal Research: Sources, Process, and Analysis* (2d ed., Carolina Academic Press 1998).

would not have been possible without their help. I am particularly grateful to Anne Abramson, Thomas Budny, Claire Toomey Durkin, Phyllis Finney, Bob Ilseman, Thomas Keefe, Kym Ogden, Victor Salas, Patricia Scott, and William Wleklinski, all of The John Marshall Law School Law Library. They not only closely reviewed drafts of many chapters, but they also undertook extensive discovery on minute points of Illinois law for the benefit of this book. For their additional comments, assistance, and support, I also thank Professors Gerald Berendt, Susan Brody, Joseph Butler, John Corkery, Joel Cornwell, Sonia Bychkov Green, Ardath Hamann, Kevin Hopkins, Gil Johnston, Walter Kendall, Maureen Straub Kordesh, Ann M. Lousin, Marie Monahan, Frank Morrissey, Sandy Olken, William Mock, Tim O'Neill, Leslie Reis, Ron Smith, David Sorkin, and Julie Spanbauer. And for their professional support, I thank Gwen Konigsfeld, Diane Gordon, and Cristine Cotter.

I thank Chief Justice Mary Ann G. McMorrow of the Illinois Supreme Court for writing the foreword to this book, and for her helpful suggestions for revisions of specific portions of the draft text. I am grateful to an army of research assistants, particularly David Hall, Ronak Joshi, Panagiota Kelali, Brian Nielson, Adam Powers, Zubaida Qazi, and Michael Roberts. I also thank many other students who helped with their comments on drafts of this work, including Michael Fenwick, Russell Kochis, Larisa Morgan, John Scott, and Dr. Janet Lee Walters.

I extend special thanks to Michael J. Faley, law clerk for the Illinois Appellate Court; John Kirkton of the Law Bulletin Publishing Company of Chicago; Rhea Ramsey of LexisNexis; Ellen Schanzle-Haskins, Director and Deputy Clerk for the Illinois Court of Claims; Bill Dineen, of the Cook County Forest Preserve District; and Lori Schneider of the Day Care Action Council. I also thank Howard Suskin of Jenner & Block, with whom I presented a full-day training program on "An Effective Approach to Legal Writing and Research."

I wish to thank my legal research and writing colleagues across the country. For their help on this book, I wish to acknowledge Barbara Busharis, Charles Calleros, Maureen Collins, Darby Dickerson,

Bryan Garner, Mark Giangrande, Peter Jan Honigsberg, Joseph Kimble, Terri LeClerq, Sue Liemer, Suzanne Rowe, Amy Sloan, and Christopher Wren.

I also extend my gratitude to the institutions that enabled me to write this book, including the Chicago Historical Society, the Chicago Public Library, The John Marshall Law School and Chicago Bar Association Law Library, the Illinois Supreme Court Law Library, the Hawaii Supreme Court Law Library, and the University of Hawaii Law School Law Library.

I am extremely grateful to my partner, David Austin, for his constant support and encouragement.

Any errors in the book are mine alone.

Mark E. Wojcik
July 2003

A Note on Citation Format

The citation format for sources found in the footnotes for each chapter largely follow the second edition of the *ALWD Citation Manual*, a book written by Dean Darby Dickerson and the Association of Legal Writing Directors. This manual is far easier to use than *The Bluebook*, and those reading the citations will seldom notice that they follow the *ALWD Citation Manual* instead. Experienced lawyers who have not yet seen the *ALWD Citation Manual* should make a point of getting a copy – its rules are familiar and the format is easy to use.

Persons who need to use *The Bluebook* citation manual can find in Chapter 11 a comparison of the citation formats of common primary and secondary law sources.

Illinois Legal Research

Chapter 1

Starting Out

I. Introduction

Legal research must be efficient, thorough, and accurate. This will be true whether you are an expert or a novice in the law library. Your clients deserve nothing less.

Learning research is like learning to ride a bicycle – you will really learn only when you try to do it. You can read all you like, but until you put your knowledge to the test you will never really learn the skills of research. As Charles Calleros correctly observes: "Effective research skills are the product of long hours in the library, for which no primer on research can substitute."[1]

This chapter first describes some of the differences you may find between research done in an academic setting and research done for clients. It then shares ten areas that you should consider before you even enter the law library to begin your research. It helps you begin the process of developing research terms and using them effectively when you consult various primary and secondary sources. And it discloses the "most overlooked research resource in the law library."

---

1. Charles R. Calleros, *Legal Method and Legal Writing* 172 (4th ed., Aspen L. & Bus. 2002).

II. Some Differences between Research for Legal Writing Classes and Research for Real Clients

There are three main differences between research done in law firms and research done as a law student.

First, law students, without the pressure of billing for the time they spend researching, may spend much more time researching an issue than they ever could afford to spend if they were in practice. Even though clients know that they must pay for the time that an attorney spends doing legal research, there is usually some limit as to what clients will pay. Most clients will not pay for 100 hours of research that should have only taken an hour. For some new researchers, some of the time spent in research is due to inefficient research techniques and unfamiliarity with many substantive areas of the law. As you do more research, however, you will naturally find that you become more efficient.

Second, law students who receive "free" computer passwords for computer research services such as Westlaw, LexisNexis, or Loislaw may not realize how much these services may cost when they are no longer free. Clients will not willingly pay for expensive computerized research if the same research could have been done in books sitting on the attorneys' shelves. Therefore, students must also be familiar with the sources that are readily available in print or on reliable sites on the Internet.

Third, if a student researcher misses an important case or statute, there will usually not be any real-life consequences to that failure. In the practice of law, however, the failure to find a relevant legal authority can result in a client losing the case.

III. Starting Your Research

A. Determine the Parameters of the Assignment

In law practice, one of the most important first steps in any research assignment arises before you ever enter a law library. This first step is to identify the parameters of the assignment. Although this may seem like an obvious first step, a researcher who fails to determine the scope and limits of an assignment is headed for almost certain trouble.

Here are ten areas of concern that will help new associates and law clerks determine the scope and limits of a research assignment.

1. *Time.* When is the assignment due? Do you have 30 days or 30 hours to do the research and write a memorandum of law? Is there a statute of limitations that is about to expire?
2. *Client.* Who is the client? Do you represent the buyer or the seller? Will the time you spend on research and writing be billed to a particular file? Is your research something that will benefit more than one client, so that you should split your billable research time between two or more clients?[2] Does your "client" have a corporate parent?
3. *Format.* What format should the final product have? Should you write an opinion letter, an internal office memorandum, or a memorandum of law to file with the court? Is the research for an appellate brief or a law review article that a senior partner is writing? Did a partner ask you merely to

---

2. Researchers should not make the ethical mistake of "double-billing" separate clients for research that may benefit more than one client. Those costs should be shared, not doubled. See e.g. ABA Formal Ethics Op. 93–379. And researchers who are doing work on a *pro bono* case should not make the ethical mistake of treating the case as somehow being "less important" than work done for a paying client. Each client is entitled to the best services you can provide.

find a statute or a few cases "on point" for a brief that must be filed with the U.S. Court of Appeals for the Seventh Circuit? Or does the partner want you to write a more formal memorandum of law that the firm will use to analyze the strengths and weaknesses of a case before deciding to file a complaint?
4. *Jurisdiction.* Does the research problem involve the law of Illinois or that of another state? Is the matter one for state or federal court? Is the matter even before a court, or is it before an administrative agency? And if the matter is in Illinois state court, which district of the Illinois Appellate Court would be binding if there was a conflict between the appellate districts?
5. *Scope.* Is anyone else working on this file now? Is another associate working on another issue in the case? Was work previously done on this file? Are you limited to any particular areas of research? Are you limited to any particular legal theories to prosecute or defend the case? Has someone in the firm worked on the same or similar legal issue in another case? Are copies of research memoranda available from that earlier case? Is there a "research file" with relevant cases, statutes, and regulations? If there is such a research memorandum or research file, how has the law developed since the time that research was done? Or has this particular client been involved in similar matters that other law firms may have handled? Do you have access to research that those other firms may have done?
6. *Facts.* What are the facts of the case? Do the facts already suggest one or more legal theories that you should research? Where can you learn additional facts about the case? Do you have access to the full case file? How should you confirm that the facts given to you are correct and complete? How can you acquire any additional facts that you might need? Do you have authority to contact the client directly to acquire any additional information or documentation that you may need for your research? Do the facts suggest that

other parties should be involved in the matter, either as an additional party to litigation or a business transaction?
7. *Hints.* Does the attorney who gave you the research assignment have any suggestions about specific research sources you should consult? Is there a particular treatise or law review article that can give you the necessary background of the legal issues and initial citations to helpful legal authorities? Does the attorney who gave you the assignment have any particular suggestions about other effective research methods you should try? Is there a "looseleaf service" you should know about?
8. *Methods.* Will the client pay for the use of computerized research services such as Westlaw or LexisNexis? Should research be done manually to save these costs? Should you start with the statutes, or with some secondary sources that may explain the larger context of a problem?
9. *Discovery.* If this is a litigation matter, has discovery already commenced? How is it progressing? How are you keeping track of the number of interrogatories, document production requests, and depositions? If your research be easier if you are sure of certain facts, should you consider drafting a request to admit facts or a request to admit the genuineness of a certain document? If litigation has not yet commenced, can you nonetheless begin the process of discovery through formal or informal means?
10. *Anything Else?* When the attorney finishes giving an assignment to you, ask if there is anything else you should know about the case or the client. Often that simple question will lead to surprising answers that will be of great assistance to you in your research. It may also save you tremendous amounts of grief, and it is a question that you might consider asking more than once. One lawyer who worked all weekend on a research project learned on Monday morning that the case had settled the previous Friday. Not only had she lost a weekend, but she could not bill the research hours expended on a case that had been settled.

You may find additional areas of concern as you start taking notes on the results of your research. But you will also find that your research can be more directed and efficient if you have first set the parameters of your legal research. When you turn in the results of your research, it will also be important to disclose the parameters under which you worked. If you did not find the result that you needed to find, you may have to expand one or more of your initial research parameters.

B. Create a List of Research Terms

Once you have set the parameters of your research project, a useful second step is to create – in writing – a list of possible research terms. Many researchers overlook this step, or do it only mentally without writing down the terms being used. But effective researchers find this to be an essential step because it causes you to think expansively about possible research terms, and also because you can later use the written list of terms as a checklist when doing your research.

First, the process of writing down research terms stimulates creative thinking about research terms. For example, if you are doing research for a product liability case, writing down the word "chair" may cause you to also write down "furniture," "table," or any number of other words. Writing down "products liability" may cause you to write down "torts," "negligence," or another area of law. And writing down "manufacturer" may cause you to remember to do research on the "seller." These associated words may all be used as possible research terms.[3]

As you are considering the facts, it is useful to explore the following familiar categories:

---

3. A useful tool for generating research terms is a legal thesaurus, such as William C. Burton, *Burton's Legal Thesaurus* (3d ed., McGraw-Hill Companies 2001).

- **Who?** Who are the parties to the transaction or litigation? Who is not a party? Are you sure that know all of the parties involved? Does the research involve third-party beneficiaries, or third-party payers such as an insurance company? If your parties are corporations or another form of business entity, is there potential personal liability for the business owners? Is there a parent corporation? Is there a government agency involved (or potentially so) in this issue? In addition to determining who the parties are, you might also consider who the witnesses might be if it is a litigation matter. If the matter involves a transaction, you might ask who else will benefit from the transaction.
- **What?** What is the specific nature of the legal problem to be researched? What is the subject matter of the problem? What is it that the parties hope to accomplish?
- **Where?** You must know the jurisdiction for your research. This is not just "Illinois," but something more specific. Which district of the Illinois Appellate Court is controlling for the area? Did the events you are researching take place on federal land? Is there an applicable local ordinance? You must also learn specifics about where any important things took place. For example, did the incident occur in the store's parking lot or on the public sidewalk? Was it in a restaurant or someone's home?
- **When?** When did the events take place? Did the applicable statute of limitations expire? For how long has this problem been around? What events in the past have already transpired? And as long as we're asking about time, when does the client need an answer on this problem? And how far back should you go with your research?
- **Why?** Why did your client do what she did? Why did the other side do what they did? And why are we doing this research now? What result is our client looking for? Is your client looking for monetary damages, injunctive relief, or a declaratory judgment?
- **How?** For the client, what process or method was involved in the issue that you are now researching? And as long as we're

asking the question "how," how should you do your research? What format should the final research project take?

Second, the list of terms that you generate can be used as a checklist with the various sources that you may consult. Seldom does a legal researcher have sustained periods of time to devote to only a single research project. The written list of research terms helps researchers return quickly to the heart of a research project by recalling what terms have already been explored.

When you are generating search terms, you should consider those familiar questions of "who, what, where, when, why, and how" that we discussed in this section. In most cases, you should try to generate search terms in each of those categories.

C. Create a List of Research Sources

After you determine the parameters of your assignment and develop an initial list of research terms, a useful third step is to consider the possible sources that you will consult. Does your research problem involve statutes, administrative regulations, or judicial decisions? Might it involve an international treaty, such as the Convention on the International Sale of Goods? Should you consult special texts, such as form books or continuing legal education materials that might be available on the specific issue? Is the issue one that you are familiar with already, or should you find a legal encyclopedia or bar journal article that explains the general background of the particular subject matter? Should you consult law review articles that may not only give citations to leading authorities, but may also explain or criticize particular rules of law in ways that may be helpful to your legal research and client advocacy?

Researchers should create a written list of sources that they intend to consult. Highly efficient researchers will use this list in conjunction with the list of research terms that they generated for a particular problem. Another method that effective legal researchers may use is to combine those two lists into a chart. On one side of the page you can write a list of your best research terms. Across the top of the page you can write the primary and secondary sources that you consult.[4] You can then use the chart simply to "check off" that you have looked up a particular term in a particular source. More effectively (and with enough room on the sheet of paper), you can briefly describe the results of your research with a particular term in a particular source.

Creating this type of a research chart on your laptop computer may allow you to organize and arrange the results of your research, but you must take care that you do not spend more time "organizing" your computerized chart than you spend actually doing research!

With larger research projects, such as research for an appellate brief or a law review article, you may also benefit from using an index card system to keep track of your research. On the top of each card you can write the name of the source. (If you use proper citation format when doing this initial step, you will also save yourself time later when you are writing.) You can organize the cards alphabetically, and keep track of the results of your research on each card. You can also periodically review the entire stack of cards to see how your research is progressing, and in which direction.[5]

One of the worst ways to keep track of your research is to make a single list on a sheet of paper that leaves you no room to take notes, and no room to organize the results of your research. But even this is better than no system at all. I remember one researcher whose "system" was to place blank "post-it" notes on particular pages of the

---

  4. This system is adapted from a suggestion by Peter Jan Honigsberg, Professor and Director of the Legal Research and Writing Program at the University of San Francisco School of Law, who encourages students to use a grid (the "Honigsberg Grid") to organize the results of legal research. You can read more about this suggestion, and see an example of it being used, in Peter Jan Honigsberg, *Legal Research, Writing and Analysis* 117–18 (Barbri Group/Thompson Co. 2002).
  5. A good description of "bibliographic check cards" can be found in Peter Cinch, *Using a Law Library: A Student's Guide to Legal Research Skills* 288–89 (2d ed., Blackstone Press 2001).

books he was using. Imagine the dismay he felt one day when his library books were reshelved and the post-it notes removed. Another researcher made copies or printouts of every potentially relevant case and secondary authority he found. Soon the stack of papers was more than two feet high. All of that paper ended up in the garbage, because it became impossible to find the particular case or source in that mountain of paper. An effective system of taking research notes would have saved a lot of lost time (and paper!).

IV. The Most Overlooked Research Resource in the Law Library

Beginning researchers are sometimes reluctant to ask for help in developing search terms or in identifying research resources. They may forget that the reference librarian is a trained professional who is there to help. Reference librarians are usually licensed lawyers with specialized knowledge and training about effective use of the research materials. If you can engage the help of the reference librarian without disclosing client confidences, then you will have tapped into the most overlooked research resource in the law library.

When asking questions of the law librarian, you should ask more than just a "directional" question such as "Where are the Restatements?" The reference librarian can answer that question for you, of course, but you can also get an answer to that question by using the library catalog and your brain. You should try to ask questions of the law librarians that will tap into their tremendous knowledge and experience. For example, you might be able to show them the list of sources that you consulted and the list of research terms that you used with those sources. You can ask what sources you missed, or whether your search terms are too narrow or too broad. You can use the skills of the reference librarian to get a feel of when you are finished with your legal research, or at least when you have done enough research to start writing.

V. Ethical Duties of Legal Research

You have ethical duties to do legal research for your clients, and to engage the help of experienced co-counsel when you are in unfamiliar legal territory. As provided by Rule 1.1 of the Illinois Rules of Professional Conduct:

    A. A lawyer shall provide competent representation to a client. Competent representation requires the legal knowledge, skill, thoroughness and preparation necessary for the representation.

    B. A lawyer shall not represent a client in a legal matter in which the lawyer knows or reasonably should know that the lawyer is not competent to provide representation, without the association of another lawyer who is competent to provide such representation.

A lawyer must also do legal research to be sure that the claims to be advanced are viable ones under Illinois law. As stated by Rule 1.2(f)(2) of the Illinois Rules of Professional Conduct: "In the representation of a client, a lawyer shall not...advance a claim or defense the lawyer knows is unwarranted under existing law, except that the lawyer may advance such claim or defense if it can be supported by a good-faith argument for an extension, modification, or reversal of existing law." As we will see in Chapter 6, there is also an obligation to the court (and the client) to update all of the authorities that you cite.

Finally, lawyers also have a responsibility as officers of the court to disclose adverse authority to the tribunal. As stated by Rule 1.2(f)(3) of the Illinois Rules of Professional Conduct: "In the representation of a client, a lawyer shall not...fail to disclose that which the lawyer is required by law to reveal." In this context, Rule 3.3(a)(3) provides: "In appearing in a professional capacity before a tribunal, a lawyer shall not...fail to disclose to the tribunal legal authority in the controlling jurisdiction known to the lawyer to be directly adverse to the position of the client and not disclosed by opposing counsel." Although you do not necessarily need to disclose persuasive (non-binding) authority that goes against your position, you must disclose any binding legal authority that directly addresses your situation.

VI. Getting Off of the Research Wheel

At some point in doing your research, you may feel like a hamster on a rotating wheel. You may find yourself going over the same material again and again. Many researchers find it difficult to stop researching, and they continue to press forward in search of the elusive "magic case." An efficient researcher knows when to stop researching and start writing.

For some researchers, knowing when to stop comes with experience. For others, the point of stopping is related only to the impending deadline or sheer exhaustion from library research. It is imperative that you develop confidence in knowing when to stop researching, or at least when to start writing. The notes that you take will help to give you a good idea of when you have done enough.

It is difficult to "develop confidence" as a researcher, and particularly the confidence that you need to stop researching. One secret is to start writing before you finish your research. Once you begin writing, your further research will be targeted specifically to the information you need to finish. Many researchers find they can build their confidence by focusing their research to the specific issues they need to research.

VII. Chapter Summary

Starting any research problem involves three essential steps.

First, you must determine the parameters of your assignment. This chapter lists ten areas that you should consider when determining what those parameters are. You should also learn as much as you can about the particular research problem so that your research time is used efficiently.

Second, begin a written list of research terms that you can use in the library. A legal thesaurus can be a useful tool to supplement a list that you create on your own.

And third, make a list of the primary and secondary law sources that you intend to consult. While you may "intend" to consult a source, keeping a list is one of the easiest ways to remember which sources you actually consulted. "Keeping good notes" about your research is an essential research strategy. Find a way to organize the results of your research.

Using these steps to plan your research will allow you to make the best use of the time you spend researching. As you enter this new field of legal research, do not be afraid to ask for help from reference librarians and other knowledgeable researchers. You should not disclose client confidences with your questions, but neither should you be afraid to ask quite specific questions about the research you are doing. When in doubt, ask the reference librarian.

Additional Resources

Busharis, Barbara J. & Suzanne E. Rowe, *Florida Legal Research: Sources, Process, and Analysis* 3–11 and 111–21 (2d ed., Carolina Academic Press 2002).

Calleros, Charles R. *Legal Method and Legal Writing* 172 (4th ed., Aspen L. & Bus. 2002).

Callister, Paul D. *Working the Problem*, 91 Ill. B.J. 43 (2003).

Clinch, Peter. *Using a Law Library: A Student's Guide to Legal Research Skills* 288–89 (2d ed., Blackstone Press 2001).

Collins, Maureen B. *Choosing Authority to Illustrate Your Point*, 84 Ill. B.J. 429 (1996).

Garner, Bryan A. *The Redbook: A Manual on Legal Style* § 14.2(a), at 286 (West Group 2002).

Honigsberg, Peter Jan. *Legal Research, Writing and Analysis* 117–18 (Barbri Group/Thompson Co. 2002).

Hook, Peter A. *Law Librarians Can Help You Save Money and Do Better Research*, 90 Ill. B.J. 373 (2002).

Hutchinson, Terry C.M. *Legal Research in Law Firms* (William S. Hein & Co. 1994) (volume 19 of the Legal Research Guide Series).

Neumann, Richard K., Jr. *Legal Reasoning and Legal Writing: Structure, Strategy, and Style* 3–14 and 119–34 (4th ed., Aspen L. & Bus. 2001).

Smith-Butler, Lisa. *Cost Effective Legal Research*, 18(2) Legal Reference Services Q. 61 (2000).

Thar, Anne E. *Ten Tips for the Newly Admitted*, 88 Ill. B.J. 105 (2000).

Wellford, Robin S. *Legal Reasoning, Writing, and Persuasive Argument* 1–8 (LexisNexis 2002).

Wojcik, Mark E. *Ten Tips for Starting Your Research Right*, 91 Ill. B.J. 359 (2003).

Chapter 2

The Illinois Constitution

I. Introduction

The state constitution provides the structure and authority of state government. The constitution establishes the procedures to elect government officials and delineates the balance of power between the various branches of state government.[1] Researchers must not forget the state constitution because laws enacted in violation of the state constitution cannot be enforced.[2] Although many provisions of the state constitution receive the same level of scrutiny as the federal constitution,[3] the Illinois Constitution may often provide a higher level of protection than the U.S. Constitution.[4] Additionally, the Illinois Constitution may explicitly identify rights that the federal constitution only implies, such as the right to privacy.[5] As to

---

1. Ill. Const. art. II, § 1.
2. *Cf. Arangold Corp. v. Zehnder*, 718 N.E.2d 191, 197 (Ill. 1999).
3. *See e.g. Jarabe v. Industrial Comm'n*, 666 N.E.2d 1, 3 (Ill. 1996).
4. *See e.g. People v. Mitchell*, 650 N.E.2d 1014, 1017 (Ill. 1995) ("We acknowledge that we are not bound to follow the Supreme Court's interpretation of Federal constitutional law. Indeed, this court has often stated that we may construe provisions of our State constitution to provide more expansive protections than the comparable Federal constitutional provisions.").
5. Ill. Const. art. I, § 6.

some of these rights, however, some courts have held that they are only "hortatory" and thus unenforceable.[6]

Although constitutional law supplies some of the most interesting issues in legal study and litigation, state constitutional legal research is often overlooked.[7] This chapter attempts to remedy that deficiency by providing leads on constitutional legal research and by sharing some bits of Illinois legal history.

A person doing research for a case involving the state constitution must:

- Find the relevant provision of the Illinois Constitution;
- Read it carefully and determine its content and effect;
- Find judicial decisions that interpret or apply the constitutional provision;
- Find other authorities that may clarify or criticize a particular provision[8]; and
- Consult published proceedings of the Constitutional Convention ("ConCon") to seek insights on any ambiguous provisions.

Researchers may also compare particular constitutional provisions to similar provisions in the constitutions of other states. While courts may not be particularly persuaded by the rulings of other

---

6. *See e.g. Wood v. Allstate Ins. Co.*, 21 F.3d 741, 743–44 (7th Cir. 1994); *Acuff v. IBP, Inc.*, 77 F. Supp. 2d 914, 919 (C.D. Ill. 1999) (despite the mandatory nature of the language in article I, section 12, that every person shall find a remedy in the law for all injuries and wrongs, the Illinois courts have held that the section does not mandate the creation of a new remedy where one does not already exist); Elmer Gertz, *Hortatory Language in the Preamble and Bill of Rights of the 1970 Constitution*, 6 John Marshall J. Prac. & P. 217 (1973).

7. Cf. Laurel Wendt, *Illinois Legal Research Manual* 1 (Butterworth Legal Publishers 1988).

8. *See e.g.* Ann Lousin, *The 1970 Illinois Constitution: Has It Made a Difference?*, 8 N. Ill. U.L. Rev. 571 (1988); Michael P. Seng & Michael R. Booden, *Judicial Enforcement of the Right to an Equal Education in Illinois*, 12 N. Ill. U.L. Rev. 45 (1991).

state courts interpreting their own constitutions, researching similar provisions from other jurisdictions can produce highly persuasive legal authorities and stimulate new thinking about constitutional litigation in our own state.

II. Illinois before Statehood

A. First Peoples

There is much that the current citizens of Illinois do not know about the first peoples who lived here. For example, many do not know that the largest pyramid outside Egypt was built in Illinois – in the area now known as Cahokia, near the confluence of the Missouri, Illinois, and Mississippi Rivers.[9] The remains of this pyramid are a great testimony to the lost Mississippian civilization that once thrived here.[10]

The recorded history of Illinois begins as early as 1634, when French explorers arrived in this area and first referred to the Native Americans of Illinois.[11] Europeans first made contacts with these Native Americans, the Illinois, around 1673.[12] The Illinois, a confederation of Algonquian peoples, called themselves "Illini" or "Iliniwek," meaning "the men,"[13] and consisted of several independent American Indian tribes.[14] They included the Kaskaskia, Peoria,

---

9. Judith Nies, *Native American History* 1 (Ballentine Books 1996).
10. *See id.*
11. Emily J. Blasingham, *The Illinois Indians, 1634–1800: A Study in Depopulation* 8 (Ph.D. dissertation, Indiana Univ. 1956) (microformed on Univ. Microfilms).
12. *Id.* at 9.
13. Otis Louis Miller, *Indian-White Relations in the Illinois Country, 1789 to 1818* 3 (Ph.D. dissertation, St. Louis Univ. 1972) (microformed on Univ. Microfilms).
14. Blasingham, *supra* note 11, at 7.

Michigamea, Tamoroa, and Cahokia.[15] In the 1680s, the Haudenosaunee (Iroquois) tribe attacked the Illinois.[16] Though badly beaten, the Illinois remained in this area under the protection of the French until the turn of the century.[17] However, the next century would see the Illinois embroiled in continuous warfare[18] and in 1832, the Illinois settled first in Kansas and later, in 1867, moved to the Indian Territory.[19]

Some recent scholarship has begun to identify historical evidence that the Haudenosaunee (Iroquois) Great Law of Peace was one of the examples (along with English and other European precedents) that influenced Benjamin Franklin, Thomas Jefferson, John Adams, and Thomas Paine in the Articles of Confederation and the Constitution.[20] More research needs to be done on this topic.

B. French Claims

The French were the first Europeans to reach Illinois, and they gave us the name "Illinois."[21] Illinois was ostensibly under French rule from 1682 to 1763.

In the early days of Illinois, the French settlers were said to have "little need of courts as they were quiet, peace loving people, owning little property over which controversies might arise, and being

---

15. *See e.g.* Lois A. Carrier, *Illinois: Crossroads of a Continent* 4 (U. Ill. Press 1998).
16. Bill Yenne, *The Encyclopedia of North American Indian Tribes* 77 (Bison Books Corp. 1986).
17. *Id.*
18. Miller, *supra* note 13, at 4.
19. Yenne, *supra* note 16, at 77.
20. *See e.g.* Bruce E. Johansen, *Debating Democracy: Native American Legacy of Freedom* 8–11, 21–29 (Clear Light Publishers 1998). For more information on the Illinois Native Americans, visit the MuseumLink Illinois website at http://www.museum.state.il.us/muslink/nat_amer/post/htmls/il.html.
21. *See* Carrier, *supra* note 15, at 9, 13.

quite willing to accept any rules prescribed by the magistrates and priests."[22] Of course, we do not know if this was really the view of the settlers, or whether it was merely the opinion of the "magistrates and priests." However, what is certain is that the need for a more formal court system developed as the population of the state increased. At some point, villagers began bringing grievances to a "commandant," whose functions included those similar to that of a judge.[23] His decisions could be appealed to a "major commandant" in Fort Chartres or Kaskaskia.[24] In capital cases, further appeal could be made to the Superior Council of Louisiana.[25]

In 1726, one of the first formal courts organized in the territory of Illinois was the Court of Audience of the Royal Jurisdiction of Illinois, which was comprised of a judge, a royal attorney, and a clerk.[26] The court held sessions at Fort Chartres and Kaskaskia through the end of the French governance of Illinois.[27]

C. English Claims

After the French and Indian War, which was the American part of the seven years' war between England and France,[28] France gave up its possessions in North America in the 1763 Treaty of Paris. England then assumed control over the land, but kept that control only for a short time. English attempts to establish a common law judicial system were unsuccessful.[29] Lieutenant Colonel Wilkens, the commandant of Fort Chartres, appointed seven men to sit as a civil tribunal, "but they were untrained and incompetent and the people

---

22. Bernita J. Davies & Francis J. Rooney, *Research in Illinois Law* 21 (Oceana Publications 1954).
23. *Id.*
24. *Id.*
25. *Id.*
26. *Id.*
27. *Id.*
28. *See* Carrier, *supra* note 15, at 19.
29. Davies & Rooney, *supra* note 22, at 21.

distrusted the common law which had superseded the Custom of Paris, in force during the French period."[30] The unhappiness of the people was reportedly at such a high level that in 1774 the British Parliament actually restored the French legal system.[31]

In August of 1775, a royal proclamation held the colonies to be in a state of rebellion.[32] The War of Independence soon followed, and the former colonies then came into possession of land previously claimed by England.

D. Illinois as Part of Virginia

In 1778, George Rogers Clark took possession of Kaskaskia in the name of Virginia, and until 1784, the Commonwealth of Virginia claimed a large part of what is now Illinois.[33] Clark established a common law court that was more popular than the one attempted by the English.[34]

According to some other maps, the northern parts of Illinois were also claimed by Connecticut.[35] But "defending and governing a distant and sparsely settled wilderness was no easier for the Virginians than it had been for the English or the French."[36] In 1783, Virginia authorized its representatives to the U.S. Congress to transfer Virginia's rights to the United States.[37] Its representatives at the time were Samuel Hardy, Arthur Lee, and future presidents Thomas Jefferson and James Monroe. These four men transferred Virginia's

---

30. *Id.*
31. *Id.*
32. *See The New Webster's International Encyclopedia* 295 (Michael D. Harkey, ed., Trident Press Intl. 1991).
33. *See e.g.* Carrier, *supra* note 15, at 32, 41.
34. *See* Davies & Rooney, *supra* note 22, at 21.
35. Charles Kendall Adams & William P. Trent, *A History of the United States* 178 (Allyn & Bacon 1913).
36. Carrier, *supra* note 15, at 32.
37. 11 Hening's Statutes at Large 326, *reprinted in* 1 Ill. Comp. Stat. 25 (Lexis 2001); *see also* Carrier, *supra* note 15, at 32.

claims to the United States in 1784.[38] The federal Congress passed a Land Ordinance Act in 1785, which produced the Northwest Ordinance two years later.[39]

E. The Northwest Ordinance of 1787

For the land north of the Ohio River and East of the Mississippi, the Congress of the Confederation enacted the "Northwest Ordinance," which set up a government for the Northwest Territory and outlawed slavery there: "There shall be neither slavery nor involuntary servitude in the said Territory, otherwise than in the punishment of crime whereof the party shall be convicted." The Northwest Ordinance was enacted on July 13, 1787 and confirmed by an Act of Congress on August 7, 1789.[40] In addition to the prohibition on slavery, it also established rules of inheritance and allowed the governor and a court consisting of three judges to "adopt and publish" criminal and civil laws "as may be necessary and best suited to the circumstances of the district" until a legislature could be organized. The three-judge court could promulgate these laws only with the assent of the governor.[41]

In addition to establishing a government for the area, the Northwest Ordinance declared a series of rights that were to "forever remain unalterable." These rights included such matters as the freedom of worship, the benefit of the writ of habeas corpus, and a right to trial by jury. The Ordinance also provided that "[t]he utmost good faith shall always be observed toward the Indians; their lands and property shall never be taken from them without their consent; and, in their property, rights, and liberty, they shall never be invaded or disturbed, unless in just and lawful wars authorized by

---

38. 11 Hening's Statutes at Large 571, *reprinted in* 1 Ill. Comp. Stat. 27 (Lexis 2001).
39. *See* Carrier, *supra* note 15, at 32.
40. The U.S. Constitution had entered into effect on March 4, 1789.
41. *See* Davies & Rooney, *supra* note 22, at 21.

Congress; but laws founded in justice and humanity, shall from time to time be made for preventing wrongs being done to them, and for preserving peace and friendship with them."[42]

The ordinance allowed the region to be divided into separate territories. Once a territory had a sufficient population of free inhabitants, it could petition Congress to become a state.[43] The new state would then be "on an equal footing with the original States in all respects whatsoever...."[44] The Northwest Territory eventually would eventually become the states of Illinois, Indiana, Ohio, Michigan, Wisconsin and part of Minnesota.

F. The Territory of Illinois (1809)

The federal law creating the Territory of Illinois entered into effect on March 1, 1809.[45] At that time, Congress also established the city of Kaskaskia on the Mississippi River as the territorial capital.[46]

III. Illinois as a State

A. The First Illinois Constitution (1818)

The U.S. Congress approved a law on April 18, 1818 to enable the people of the Illinois territory to form a constitution and state government.[47] The first state constitution for Illinois was adopted after a Constitutional Convention in August 1818 in Kaskaskia, the first

---

42. Northwest Ordinance, art. 3.
43. There is some historical debate as to whether Illinois had a sufficient number of free inhabitants to become a state. *See e.g.* Carrier, *supra* note 15, at 40.
44. Northwest Ordinance, art. 5.
45. 2 Stat. 514, 514–15 (1809).
46. *Id.* §8, 2 Stat. at 516; *see also* Carrier, *supra* note 15, at 34.
47. 3 Stat. 428 (1818).

state capital.[48] 9 On December 3, 1818, President Monroe signed the act that made Illinois the 21st State.[49] That date, December 3, 1818, is the State's official birthday.

The first Constitution of 1818 vested the greatest powers in the legislature.[50] It gave so much power to the Illinois state legislature that the Governor could not even veto legislation on his own. Instead, all legislation, before it became law, was sent to a council consisting of "the governor...and the judges of the supreme court, or a major part of them, together with the governor" who would review and revise laws that were about to be passed by the General Assembly.[51] The Governor and justices of the Illinois Supreme Court were not to be paid any salary for this work,[52] an idea that may have been designed to ensure that they would not spend much time reviewing legislation. If the council did revise some part of the legislation, the General Assembly could override that revision by a simple majority of both houses.[53] If the council did not revise the legislation, the justices of the Illinois Supreme Court would have had a hard time declaring unconstitutional the very same legislation that they themselves had already reviewed and approved.[54]

The first Chief Justice of the Illinois Supreme Court was Joseph Phillips, a resident of Randolph County and a veteran of the war of 1812.[55] Justice Phillips served from October 9, 1818 until July 4, 1822, when he resigned to become a candidate for governor.[56] He

---

48. 9 Kaskaskia, the first capital, was located on the Mississippi River. A flood wiped out the city in 1881, leaving only "Kaskaskia Island." That island is now the only part of Illinois that is west of the Mississippi River.
49. *See* Carrier, *supra* note 15, at 45.
50. *See* Robert P. Howard, *Illinois: A History of the Prairie State* 114 (William B. Eerdmans Publg. Co. 1972).
51. Ill. Const. art. III, § 19 (1818).
52. *Id.*
53. *Id.*; Howard, *supra* note 50, at 114.
54. Howard, *supra* note 50, at 114.
55. John Clayton, *The Illinois Fact Book and Historical Almanac (1673–1968)* 97 (Southern Ill. Univ. Press 1970).
56. *Id.*

lost that race and moved back to Tennessee.[57] The first Associate Justices of the Illinois Supreme Court were Thomas C. Browne, John Reynolds, and William P. Forster, who was elected as an Associate Justice but never actually served.[58]

The first state constitution prohibited the introduction of slavery and involuntary servitude, except as punishment for crimes.[59] However, the framers did not have the courage to ban slavery altogether. Until 1824, Illinois tolerated slavery at the Lick Reservation Salt Works that were "leased to certain wealthy Kentuckians, who work them by their slaves, and could not work them, if their slaves should become free by being sent into Illinois."[60] It also listed a number of specific rights, including the rights of juries in libel cases to decide not only the facts of the case but also the applicable law.[61] A schedule to the constitution limited the right to vote to white male residents over the age of 21.[62] It also mandated that the general assembly "enact such laws as may be necessary and proper to prevent the practice of dueling."[63]

The text of the first Illinois Constitution was included in the first book of laws printed in the State of Illinois.[64] It was also published

---

57. *Id.*
58. *Id.*
59. Ill. Const. art. VI, §1 (1818).
60. George Churchill, *Letter of George Churchill of Madison County [Illinois] to Mr. Swift Eldred, Warren [Connecticut]*, reprinted in 11 J. Ill. State Hist. Soc'y 64, 64–65 (1918). Mr. Churchill wrote further that: "On the whole, although the Constitution does not exactly suit me, yet there is nothing to deter, and everything to encourage and stimulate the Yankees to emigrate hither [to Illinois]. Slavery is so far excluded, that hardly any slaveholder will think of settling here, especially while the Missouri Territory offers them so many advantages. Our emigrants will henceforth be composed of friends of liberty and of election by ballot." *Id.* at 65.
61. Ill. Const. art. VIII, §23 (1818).
62. Ill. Const. *Schedule* §12 (1818).
63. Ill. Const. *Schedule* §11 (1818).
64. *Laws Passed by the First General Assembly of the State of Illinois* 1 (Blackwell & Berry 1819).

separately by E. De. Krafft of Washington City, Illinois.[65] There is no official record of the first constitutional convention.[66]

When the Illinois General Assembly convened under this new constitution, its first act was to adopt the common law of England as the law of Illinois.[67] The "Act Declaring What Laws are in Force in this State" provides:

> That the common law of England, all statutes or acts of the British Parliament made in aid of the common law prior to the fourth year of the reign of King James the I. excepting the second section of the sixth chapter of XLIII. Elizabeth; the eighth chapter XIII. Elizabeth, and ninth chapter XXXVII. Henry VII. and which are of a general nature and not local to that Kingdom, shall be the rule of decision, and shall be considered as of full force, until repealed by legislative authority.

This first statute adopted by the Illinois General Assembly still occasionally appears in Illinois court decisions.[68]

In 1819, the state capital moved to Vandalia, Illinois, a city 70 miles east of St. Louis, Missouri. Citizens in other cities campaigned to move the capital to the geographic center of the state, however, and in 1833, the General Assembly allowed voters to decide whether to keep the capital in Vandalia or to move it to Alton, Jacksonville, Peoria, or Springfield.[69] The residents of Vandalia were quite determined to keep the capital in their city. In 1836, when the legislature was not in session, they tore down the wooden capitol

---

65. A copy can be found in the research library of the Chicago Historical Society.
66. Davies & Rooney, *supra* note 22, at 9. Some additional background on the first Illinois Constitutional Convention can be found in Carrier, *supra* note 15, at 40–44.
67. *See* 1819 Ill. Laws 3; Laurel Wendt, *Illinois Legal Research Manual* 126 (Butterworth Legal Publishers 1988).
68. Wendt, *supra* note 67, at 126 (citing *Torres v. Walsh*, 456 N.E.2d 601 (Ill. 1983)).
69. Jesse White, *1999–2000 Handbook of Illinois Government* 99 (1999); Carrier, *supra* note 15, at 85.

building and replaced it with a brick structure that cost $16,000.[70] Despite their efforts, however, the capital was moved to Springfield.[71] Vandalia had served as the state capital from 1819 to 1839. Abraham Lincoln, the 16th president of the United States, was a state representative at the Vandalia Statehouse. It was in that building that Lincoln's name was entered into the state rolls as a practicing attorney in 1837.[72] It was also around this time that some citizens of the northern counties of Illinois, feeling neglected by the downstate capital, petitioned Congress (unsuccessfully) to become part of Wisconsin.[73]

Although a legal system was in place, the pioneers of Illinois have been described as having little respect for formal laws and courts.[74] Lynchings and beatings by vigilante groups were used with horse thieves and other villains.[75] The early legal system, for its part, "was not well designed for the administration of justice."[76] Only seven criminal cases appeared on the docket for McLean County in 1838, although there were at least 368 civil cases.[77] When it came to criminal matters, jurors would convict strangers but not friends or relatives.[78] Murderers were often acquitted, given light sentences, or allowed to escape the state.[79] An exception to the string of acquittals arose in 1843 in Lawrence County, where a woman was hanged after she poisoned her husband.[80]

---

70. White, *supra* note 69, at 99.
71. *Id.*
72. *See* Albert A. Woldman, *Lawyer Lincoln* 23 (Carroll & Graf Publishers 1994).
73. Carrier, *supra* note 15, at 86.
74. *See* Richard J. Jensen, *Illinois: A Bicentennial History* 7 (W.W. Norton & Co. & the Am. Assn. for State and Local History 1978).
75. *Id.* at 7, 26.
76. *Id.* at 26.
77. *Id.* at 27.
78. *Id.* at 26.
79. *Id.*
80. *Id. See also* A.T. Andreas, *History of Cook County Illinois* 251–52 (A.T. Andreas 1884) (describing the 1834 acquittal of a man arraigned for killing his wife).

Springfield became the state capital in 1839. Construction on the first capitol building was completed in 1853; the renovated building is now known as "the Old State Capitol." In a building across the street, Abraham Lincoln had a law office that is now a museum depicting typical law offices, the federal district courtroom, related court offices, and meeting rooms. Lincoln also served as a state legislator, pled cases before the Illinois Supreme Court,[81] and delivered his famous anti-slavery speech in which he declared that "A House Divided Against Itself Cannot Stand."

The present state capitol building was completed in 1888.[82]

B. The Second Illinois Constitution (1848)

The political situation in Illinois had changed by 1847, when a second constitutional convention was convened. The second Illinois Constitution included a more detailed article on the judiciary, reduced the number of Supreme Court Justices from four to three, and provided for the popular election of judges rather than their appointment.[83] The Constitution also created Circuit Courts, County Courts, and Justices of the Peace.[84] The power of the Illinois Governor was increased by abolishing the Council of Revision and by giving the Governor the legislative veto. The legislature could override that veto by a simple majority vote, however, rather than the two-thirds majority which some had advocated. For those who need to conduct historical research on the Illinois Constitution, Lanphier and Walker of Springfield published the journal of the 1847 Constitutional Convention.[85]

---

81. Lincoln's first reported case before the Illinois Supreme Court was *Scammon v. Cline*, 3 Ill. 456 (1840). Other cases argued by Abraham Lincoln before the Illinois Supreme Court include *Cannon v. Kinney*, 4 Ill. 9 (1841); *Bailey v. Cromwell*, 4 Ill. 71 (1841), *Elkin v. People*, 4 Ill. 207 (1841), and *Grable v. Margrave*, 4 Ill. 372 (1842).
82. White, *supra* note 69, at 99.
83. Davies & Rooney, *supra* note 22, at 22.
84. *Id.*
85. *A Journal of the Convention Assembled at Springfield, June 7, 1847.*

C. The Third Illinois Constitution (1870)

A new constitution was proposed in 1862,[86] but it was rejected because of the extreme partisanship and distractions of the Civil War that had started in 1861.

When a new Constitutional Convention convened in 1870, members of the Illinois Woman Suffrage Association traveled to Springfield to lobby for the right to vote. Frances Elizabeth Willard told the delegates: "The idea that boys of 21 are fit to make laws for their mothers is an insult to everyone." The delegates followed the pattern set by the 15th Amendment to the U.S. Constitution, however, and drafted a document that gave the right to vote to all adult males, including African-Americans, but it did not extend that right to women or to unnaturalized foreigners.[87]

The constitution of 1870 expanded the number of Supreme Court justices to seven and authorized the creation of inferior appellate courts after 1874.[88]

Women received limited rights to vote on June 19, 1891, when the Illinois General Assembly passed a bill that entitled women to vote at any election held to elect school officials.[89] Because these elections were held at the same time as elections for other offices, women had to use separate ballots and separate ballot boxes.[90] Women were later allowed to cast ballots for trustees of the University of Illinois, and even run for that office.[91]

Another Constitutional Convention was convened in 1920. After several recesses, it produced a document that the voters of Illinois

---

86. Lanphier of Springfield published the *Journal of the Constitutional Convention of 1862.*

87. A two-volume *Debates and Proceedings of the Constitutional Convention of 1870* was published by Merritt, Springfield, 1870.

88. *See* Davies & Rooney, *supra* note 22, at 22–23.

89. *Laws of the State of Illinois,* 37th General Assembly 135 (1891).

90. *See* Mark W. Sorensen, *Ahead of Their Time: A Brief History of Woman Suffrage in Illinois,* http://alexia.lis.uiuc.edu/~sorensen/suff.html.

91. *See id.*

overwhelmingly rejected in 1922.[92] A five-volume set of proceedings from that proposed constitution was published in 1922. The Constitution of 1870 was amended several times, however, so researchers must take care to look for different versions of a particular provision.[93]

D. The Current Illinois Constitution (1970)

The current Illinois Constitution was adopted in Springfield on September 3, 1970 at the conclusion of the nine-month Illinois Constitutional Convention (known as the "Con-Con"). The voters of Illinois ratified the current constitution on December 15, 1970, and it entered into effect on July 1, 1971. The Illinois Constitution can be found in many print and electronic sources, including the *Illinois Compiled Statutes,* the *Illinois Blue Book,* and the *Handbook of Illinois Government.* Legal researchers will likely be most interested in the versions published in the annotated statutes, because those versions contain not only the text of the constitution but citations to judicial decisions and law review articles interpreting particular provisions.

Among the changes important to researchers was a requirement to produce a record of debates in the General Assembly. "Each house shall keep a journal of its proceedings and a transcript of its debates. The journal shall be published and the transcript available to the public."[94] Before this time, there was no easy way of tracking the legislative history of Illinois statutes.[95]

The Illinois Constitution has been amended ten times since it entered into effect.

    1. Legislative Article (Cutback Amendment) (1980). The first amendment eliminated cumulative ("bullet") voting and re-

---

92. Walter F. Dodd & Sue Hutchison Dodd, *Government in Illinois* 46 (U. Chicago Press 1923).
93. *See* Wendt, *supra* note 67, at 4.
94. Ill. Const. art. IV, §7(b).
95. *See e.g.* Laurel A. Wendt, *Researching Illinois Legislative Histories – A Practical Guide,* 1982 S. Ill. U. L.J. 601, 602 (1983).

duced the size of the House of Representatives from 177 to 118 members.
2. Revenue Article (Delinquent Tax Sales) (1980). The second amendment reduced the minimum redemption period to prevent abuse in scavenger sales by persons who had not paid their property taxes.
3. Bill of Rights Article (Bail and Habeas Corpus) (1982). The third amendment permitted judges to deny bail to anyone who was accused of a crime that carried a possible life sentence.
4. Bill of Rights Article (Bail and Habeas Corpus) (1986). The fourth amendment permitted judges to deny bail for felony offenses where the release of the alleged offender "would pose a real and present threat to the physical safety of any person."[96]
5. Suffrage and Elections Article (Voting Qualifications) (1988). The fifth amendment reduced the voting age from 21 to 18 and reduced the voter's Illinois residency requirement from six months to 30 days before any election, all to conform to the 26th Amendment to the U.S. Constitution.
6. Revenue Article (Delinquent Tax Sales) (1990). The sixth amendment amended the second amendment, relating to the redemption of certain properties with tax delinquencies.[97]
7. Bill of Rights Article (Crime Victim's Rights) (1992). The seventh amendment provided certain rights to crime victims.
8. Bill of Rights (Rights After Indictment) (1994). The eighth amendment replaced the right "to meet the witnesses face to face" with a right "to be confronted with the witnesses against him or her."[98]

---

96. Ill. Const. art. I, §9 (as amended Nov. 4, 1986; effective Nov. 25, 1986).

97. Ill. Const. art. IX, §8 (as amended Nov. 6, 1990; effective Nov. 26, 1990).

98. Ill. Const. art. I, §8 (added by the Seventh Amendment approved Nov. 3, 1992; effective Nov. 23, 1992).

9. Legislative Article (Effective Dates of Laws) (1994). The ninth amendment changed the effective dates of certain laws.
10. Judiciary Article (Retirement - Discipline) (1994). The tenth amendment added two citizen members to the Illinois Courts Commission, the body that hears complaints filed against judges that are filed by the Judicial Inquiry Board and decides punishment. There are also two "alternate" citizen members.[99]

West and LexisNexis each publish annotated versions of the current constitution. It is these versions that are most helpful for researchers. The annotated versions contain constitutional commentary, historical notes, cross-references to other constitutional provisions, and citations to scholarly commentary in law review and bar journal articles. Most importantly, they contain headnotes of court decisions that apply particular constitutional provisions.

The proceedings of the 1970 Illinois Constitutional Convention are available in a seven-volume set that the Illinois Secretary of State published in 1972. The volumes should be available in most Illinois law libraries.

E. Special Rules for Citing the Illinois Constitution

When you are writing about the Illinois Constitution in a sentence, you should spell out the provision instead of using the citation format.[100] For example:

> The court ruled that the plaintiffs had no standing to enforce section 20 of article I of the Illinois Constitution.

Unless you are writing about historical developments, readers will assume that you are citing the most recent version of the state

---

99. *See also* Peggy Boyer Long, *Amendment on Ballot: Non-Judges Could Sit on Judicial Commission*, 24 Ill. Issues 8 (Oct. 1998).
100. Association of Legal Writing Directors & Darby Dickerson, *ALWD Citation Manual* 100 (2d ed., Aspen Publishers 2003).

constitution. In citing the state constitution in a footnote or separate citation sentence, you need only to give the name of the constitution and a specific reference to the section (and, if appropriate, the subsection) that you are citing.[101] You do not need to include the year if you are citing to the current constitution. For example:

> "Every person shall find a certain remedy in the laws for all injuries and wrongs which he receives to his person, privacy, property or reputation." Ill. Const. art. I, § 12.

> The Illinois Constitution condemns "communications that portray criminality, depravity or lack of virtue in, or that incite violence, hatred, abuse or hostility toward, a person or group of persons by reason of or reference to religious, racial, ethnic, national or regional affiliation...." Ill. Const. art. I, § 20.

If it will assist your readers, you may also add information in a parenthetical after a citation. For example:

> Ill. Const. art. I, § 6 (Right to Privacy).

You must also include the year when citing earlier constitutions. Similarly, if you are citing constitutional provisions that may have been repealed or superseded, you should use the citation format for current constitutions but use a parenthetical to explain why the particular section is no longer in force.[102] Examples of how to cite the Illinois Constitution under the *ALWD Citation Manual* and *The Bluebook* are included in the chapter on citation. There is no appropriate short citation format for the Illinois Constitution.[103] But *id.* can be used if the previous citation was also to the Illinois Constitution.

---

101. *See id.* at 98–100.
102. *Id.* at 105.
103. *Id.* "In other words, if *id.* is not appropriate, repeat the full citation." *Id.* at 106.

IV. Chapter Summary

The Illinois Constitution establishes the structure and authority of state government. Additionally, laws enacted in violation of the state constitution cannot be enforced. Where facts warrant constitutional analysis, researchers should remember that the Illinois Constitution may provide a higher or more specific protection than the federal constitution.

Additional Resources

Carrier, Lois A. *Illinois: Crossroads of a Continent* (U. Ill. Press 1998).

Cornelius, Janet. *Constitution Making in Illinois 1818–1870* (U. Ill. Press 1972).

Davies, Bernita J., & Francis J. Rooney. *Research in Illinois Law* 9 (Oceana Publications 1954).

Dodd, Walter F., & Sue Hutchison Dodd. *Government in Illinois* 46 (U. Chicago Press 1923).

Gertz, Elmer. *Charter for a New Age: An Inside View of the Sixth Illinois Constitutional Convention* (U. Ill. Press 1980).

Gertz, Elmer. *Hortatory Language in the Preamble and Bill of Rights of the 1970 Constitution,* 5 J. Marshall. J. Prac. & Proc. 216 (1972).

Howard, Robert P. *Illinois: A History of the Prairie State* (William B. Eerdmans Publg. Co. 1972).

Jacobs, Roger F. *Statutory Law* in *Illinois Legal Research Sourcebook* 1-1 to 1-3 (Ill. Inst. for CLE 1977).

Johansen, Bruce E. *Debating Democracy: Native American Legacy of Freedom* (Clear Light Publishers 1998).

Kopecky, Frank, & Mary Sherman Harris. *Understanding the Illinois Constitution* (Ill. Bar Found. 1986).

Lousin, Ann. *The 1970 Illinois Constitution: Has It Made a Difference?*, 8 N. Ill. U.L. Rev. 571 (1988).

Mersky, Roy M. & Donald J. Dunn, *Fundamentals of Legal Research* 144–45 (8th ed., Found. Press. 2002).

Neis, Judith. *Native American History* (Ballentine Books 1996).

Nutt Carleton, Jennifer L. *Indian Law for Illinois Practitioners*, 88 Ill. B.J. 659 (2000).

Wendt, Laurel. *Illinois Legal Research Manual* 1–9 (Butterworth Legal Publishers 1998).

Witwer, Samuel W. *Introduction to the 1970 Illinois Constitution*, 1 Ill. Comp. Stat. Ann. XIX to XXIV (Smith-Hurd 1997).

Woldman, Albert A. *Lawyer Lincoln* (Carroll & Graf Publishers 1994).

Chapter 3

Illinois Judicial Decisions

I. Introduction

Reported court decisions show how courts resolved past disputes and give guidance to the public as to how similar disputes might also be resolved. Court decisions are often the starting point and finishing point of legal research, although a wise researcher will always consult the statutes, regulations, and secondary authorities that may resolve a particular legal research problem. Court decisions do not simply apply statutes enacted by the legislature or regulations promulgated by the state administrative agencies. Under the common law system, courts also interpret statutes and regulations. The courts' decisions themselves then become part of the binding law of the state. Courts also create areas of law that are not governed by statute or regulation where judge-made common law prevails.

Judicial decisions are reported, not surprisingly, in reporters. This is the name given to the series of books that publishes court decisions. There are official reporters and unofficial reporters in Illinois. There are also many state court decisions in Illinois that are said to be "unreported," much to the dismay of the practicing bar.[1] Under Rule 23 of the Illinois Supreme Court Rules, these unre-

---

1. *See e.g.* John Flynn Rooney, *Lawyers Debate What Appeals Court Leaves Unsaid*, Chicago Daily Law Bulletin, Apr. 27, 2002, at 5.

ported decisions may not be cited as authority, even if they are directly on point.[2]

This chapter reviews the structure of state courts, the reporters in which the published opinions appear, and the digests that researchers can use to access Illinois court decisions.

II. Overview of the Illinois State Court System

The state court system includes the Illinois Supreme Court, 5 judicial districts of the Illinois Appellate Court, and 22 circuit courts for the 102 counties of Illinois. It also includes the Illinois Court of Claims, although that court may be better characterized as an administrative agency or as part of the legislative branch rather than as part of the independent judiciary.

A. Illinois Supreme Court

1. Stare Decisis

Under the doctrine of *stare decisis*, the Illinois Supreme Court will generally adhere to its previous rulings, and lower state courts (the appellate courts and circuit courts) must follow and apply its holdings to new cases that have the same or similar facts.

U.S. Supreme Court Justice Antonin Scalia has described the development of the doctrine of *stare decisis* as being something like a Scrabble board, in which additional tiles are added to those previously placed on the board.[3] According to this clever analogy, new

---

2. Strangely enough, on the federal level there is now even a "reporter" to report "unreported" decisions. This reporter is called the Federal Appendix, and many lawyers are still entirely unaware that it exists.
3. Antonin Scalia, *A Matter of Interpretation: Federal Courts and the Law* 8 (Princeton U. Press 1997).

Illinois Judicial Decisions • 39

Illinois Appellate Court Districts

cases decided by the courts must find their place among the other cases previously decided by the court. Earlier cases are not ignored or discarded, just as tiles played in a Scrabble game are not discarded when a new word is made. As Justice Scalia wrote: "No rule of decision previously announced could be *erased*, but qualifications could be *added* to it."[4]

The common law depends on the doctrine of *stare decisis*, which generally holds that courts should follow the rules in earlier court decisions (unless there is a good reason not to do so). Lawyers who do not like the results or reasoning of those earlier decisions must develop facts to distinguish their case from the binding precedent. They may also be able to argue that the unfavorable part of the earlier court decision was only *dicta* that was not necessary to the resolution of the case. *Dicta* need not be followed as binding authority under the doctrine of *stare decisis*.[5] Because *dicta* is usually not labeled as such in a court opinion, many have argued that one lawyer's "*dicta*" may be another lawyer's "holding."

If they cannot distinguish the facts of their case or show that the language in question is merely *dicta*, then the lawyers must either seek a legislative solution to their problem or be prepared to appeal their case through the state court system until they have an opportunity to convince the Illinois Supreme Court to reverse its earlier holding. "A decision by the supreme court constitutes the law of the state so as to be binding until overruled by the supreme court."[6]

2. Information about the Illinois Supreme Court

The Supreme Court sits in Springfield, the state capital. The court may also sit from time to time in Chicago at the Michael A. Bilandic Building. Oral arguments are open to the public. Law students should attend at least one oral argument while they are in law school.

---

4. *Id.* (emphasis in original).
5. *See e.g. Geer v. Kadera*, 671 N.E.2d 692, 699 (Ill. 1996).
6. *Chicago Title & Trust Co. v. Vance*, 529 N.E.2d 1134, 1138 (Ill. App. 1st Dist. 1988), *appeal denied*, 535 N.E.2d 913 (Ill. 1989).

There are seven justices on the Illinois Supreme Court: three are elected from the First Judicial District (Cook County) and one each from the remaining four Judicial Districts in the state.[7] Illinois Supreme Court justices serve for terms of 10 years.[8] Additional information about the Illinois Supreme Court is available on its website, http://www.state.il.us/court/.

3. Illinois Supreme Court Opinions

Opinions from the Illinois Supreme Court are available from a number of sources, including the clerk of court, electronic sources including the court's own website,[9] and in commercial databases such as Lexis,[10] Westlaw,[11] Loislaw,[12] or the internet-based National Law Library.[13] Illinois Supreme Court opinions may also be found the old-fashioned way – in books, in the law library.

Decisions of the Illinois Supreme Court are published officially in the reporter called *Illinois Reports*. The *Illinois Reports* contain all of the Illinois Supreme Court decisions reported from the earliest history of the state until the present.[14] The West Group also publishes Illinois Supreme Court decisions in two other sources: the *Illinois Decisions* and the *North Eastern Reporter*. These two reporters are "unofficial reporters." The text of the court decision between the official and unofficial reporters will usually be identical. But if there is a conflict between the official source and the unofficial source, the

---

7. Ill. Const. art. VI, § 3.
8. Ill. Const. art. VI, § 10.
9. For more information, visit http://www.state.il.us/court/Opinions/Search.htm.
10. For more information, visit http://www.lexis.com.
11. For more information, visit http://www.westlaw.com.
12. For more information, visit http://www.loislaw.com or email info@loislaw.com.
13. For more information, visit http://www.itislaw.com.
14. The first series of that reporter includes Illinois Supreme Court cases until 1953, when the *Illinois Reports* began a second series (commonly abbreviated as "Ill. 2d").

official source will control. The main differences between the official and unofficial reporters relate to the speed of publication (unofficial reports are usually much faster) and to editorial enhancements (unofficial reports may contain more "headnotes" that assist readers).

4. How to Read a Citation

A citation to a case tells the reader exactly where a case can be found. For example, the citation *Carroll v. Paddock,* 199 Ill. 2d 16 (2002), tells the reader that the particular case can be found in volume 199 of the *Illinois Reports, Second Series,* and that the case will start on page 16. The *Illinois Reports* is the official reporter for decisions of the Illinois Supreme Court. Under Rule 6 of the Illinois Supreme Court Rules, citations to documents filed in Illinois state courts must include the citation to the official reports (and may include citations to the unofficial reports).[15]

Under the most current editions of the *Bluebook* and the *ALWD Citation Manual,* a case will be cited to the unofficial regional reporter rather than the state reporter. Thus, the same case would be cited as *Carroll v. Paddock,* 764 N.E.2d 1118 (Ill. 2002). This means that the case will be found in volume 764 of the *North Eastern Reports, Second Series,* and that the case will start on page 1118 of that reporter. You may notice that the designation of the year includes the abbreviation "Ill." This tells readers that the decision was from the Illinois Supreme Court. It was not necessary to include that abbreviation when we cited to "Ill. 2d" in the previous paragraph, because readers know that all of the decisions reported in "Ill. 2d" are from the Illinois Supreme Court.

In legal memoranda and briefs filed in court, a citation to a decision of the Illinois Supreme Court will often include the official reporter and both unofficial reporters. The citations to the unofficial reporters are often referred to as the "parallel citations." This citation, for example, includes citations to the official and both unofficial reporters:

---

15. The rule is reprinted in the ALWD Citation Manual.

Carroll v. Paddock, 199 Ill. 2d 16, 262 Ill. Dec. 1, 764 N.E.2d 1118 (2002). This citation tells readers that the case can be found in three different reporters, rather than just one. This is an important thing to remember if the particular reporter volume that you need is missing from the shelf. You can find that same decision published elsewhere. In the example here, the decision in *Carroll v. Paddock* can be found in:

(1) Volume 199 of the *Illinois Reports, Second Series,* starting at page 16;
(2) Volume 262 of the *Illinois Decisions,* at page 1; and
(3) Volume 764 of the *North Eastern Reporter, Second Series,* at page 1118.

The *Illinois Decisions* published by West reports cases from the Illinois Supreme Court and the Illinois Appellate Court. The regional reporter series *North Eastern Reporter* publishes decisions from five states: Illinois, Indiana, Ohio, New York, and Massachusetts.[16] Some novice researchers wrongly believe that because these states are grouped together, Illinois courts will consider decisions from those other states covered by the *North Eastern Reporter* to be more persuasive than decisions from other jurisdictions. The grouping of states is entirely arbitrary – for example, who would place Illinois in the "Northeastern" part of the United States? The important thing to remember is that courts afford no additional weight to persuasive authority from these jurisdictions because of the accident of being published in the same regional reporter.

5. Finding Parallel Citations

You will need to find a parallel citation when the specific book you are looking for is missing from the shelf, or if you need to include official and unofficial reporters in a case you are citing to an

---

16. The reporter called *West's Illinois Decisions* takes only the Illinois cases from the *North Eastern Reporter* and publishes them separately.

Illinois court. More information on case citation will be found in chapter 11, including a chart with sample citations that use parallel citations.

There are several ways to find a parallel citation.

- If you are using electronic legal research sources, the parallel citations are usually available at the beginning of the document, or by using the electronic updating features for the system you are using.
- Parallel citations for cases can also be found by using the print Shepard's Case Citator, a tool discussed in Chapter 6. The parallel citations will be found in parenthesis after the first time a case is listed in the reporter.
- The West reporters include "Parallel Citation Tables" in the beginning of the reporters, often on blue pages.
- The advance sheets published for West reporters also include a table of parallel citations for cases.
- Finally, there is a "National Reporter Blue Book" that includes parallel citations for all state cases reported in the United States.

B. Illinois Appellate Court

The Illinois Appellate Court is the intermediate court of review in Illinois. The Illinois Appellate Court is divided into five judicial districts rather than five separate appellate courts.[17] The First Judicial District of the Illinois Appellate Court consists only of Cook County,[18] the most populous part of the state. The rest of the state is divided into four judicial districts of "substantially equal popula-

---

17. *See e.g. Newsom v. Friedman*, 76 F.3d 813, 818 (7th Cir. 1996).
18. Ill. Const. art. VI, §2. The First Judicial District is further divided into several "divisions," which are panels of three judges. These divisions are essentially fungible, and there is no need to identify the Division of the First Judicial District. It is sufficient to identify only that the decision came from the First District.

tion."[19] As with the Illinois Supreme Court, judges are also elected to this court. A map of the five appellate judicial districts is available at http://www.state.il.us/court/AppellateCourt/Map.htm.

1. Finding Published Decisions

Decisions of the five judicial districts of the Illinois Appellate Court are published officially in the *Illinois Appellate Court Reports*.[20] Decisions are also published unofficially in the *North Eastern Reporter*, which is a regional reporter, and the *Illinois Decisions*. A citation for a decision from the Illinois Appellate Court may refer to one, two, or all three of these reporters. For example:

People v. Jones, 328 Ill. App. 3d 233, 262 Ill. Dec. 115, 764 N.E.2d 1232 (1st Dist. 2002).

In addition to the three reporters,[21] Illinois Appellate Court decisions can also be found in electronic databases such as Westlaw, LexisNexis, and the website for the Illinois Appellate Court.[22]

If you know the name of an Illinois case but not its citation, you may find the citation by using the *Shepard's Illinois Case Names Citator*. This particular citator compiles case names and citations of Illinois decisions from 1925 to the present. You can also use this citator as a research tool to learn if the parties in your case have been involved in other reported appellate litigation.

---

19. Ill. Const. art. VI, §2.
20. The first series of the *Illinois Appellate Court Reports* contains Illinois Appellate Court decisions until 1953. The second series (normally abbreviated as Ill. App. 2d) contains decisions from 1953 to 1971. The third series (normally abbreviated as Ill. App. 3d) contains decisions from 1971 to the present.
21. The three reporters are (1) the Illinois Appellate Reports; (2) Illinois Decisions; and (3) the Northeastern Reporter.
22. http://www.state.il.us/court/AppellateCourt/default.htm. In addition to carrying the text of opinions, the court's official website includes general information about the court, its justices, and the docket of upcoming oral arguments

2. Illinois Appellate Court Decisions before 1935 Are Not Binding

Illinois Appellate Court decisions were not binding until 1935, when the legislature amended the Illinois Courts Act.[23] The fact that certain appellate court decisions are not binding is an obscure piece of legal trivia, and very few researchers know it (at least until now). But one day, you may find yourself in litigation where the only authority cited by the other side is an Illinois Appellate Court decision before 1935. If that happens, simply inform the court that the decision is not binding.

Another quirk is that many decisions before 1935 were published only as "abstracts." If you need to find the full opinions on which these abstracts were based, you can find them in a limited number of law libraries, such as the law library for The John Marshall Law School.

3. "Unpublished" Decisions and Rule 23

Rule 23 of the Illinois Supreme Court Rules allows the court to decide cases without giving them any value as legal precedent, except for very limited purposes of supporting arguments of double jeopardy, *res judicata*,[24] collateral estoppel, or law of the case.[25] It was thought that giving the courts the authority to decide cases in this way would clear up a backlog of appeals and allow the court to focus on cases that are more important. It was also thought that the increase in litigation was simply creating too many cases for Illinois lawyers to read. For these reasons of judicial economy and of alleviating the burden of "keeping current" with the law, some decisions were allowed to be "unpublished."

---

23. *See e.g. Chicago Title & Trust Co. v. Vance*, 529 N.E.2d 1134, 1138 (Ill. App. 1st Dist. 1988), *appeal denied*, 535 N.E.2d 913 (Ill. 1989).

24. *See* Barbara Anderson Gimble, *The Res Judicata Doctrine Under Illinois and Federal Law*, 88 Ill. B.J. 404 (2000).

25. 134 Ill. 2d R. 23. The current version of the rule is published separately in an annual pamphlet of Illinois Supreme Court Rules and also as part of the Illinois statutes.

The term "unpublished" is a misnomer, however, as the decisions are actually published electronically on Westlaw, Lexis, and even the court's own website.[26] Although a competent researcher may find these "unpublished" decisions, under Illinois Supreme Court Rule 23 they may not be cited as authority to courts or administrative agencies.[27] The constitutionality of prohibiting citations to unpublished decisions has been challenged in other jurisdictions.[28] At some point, there may be a similar challenge in Illinois to the prohibition of citing unpublished cases.[29] Defenders of unpublished decisions claim that they allow the court to do its work faster without concern for the precedential value of its decisions. By making it impossible to cite these decisions as authority, the courts can reach their decisions more quickly. However, this argument only encourages "sloppy" court decisions.

Critics of the prohibition on citing unpublished decisions also argue that the very idea of having a court issue a decision that you cannot then cite as authority runs entirely contrary to the spirit and tradition of the common law system.[30] It is particularly frustrating to

---

26. http://www.state.il.us/court/Opinions/Search.htm. A recent change to the website allows individuals to receive email notices of new decisions. On the federal level, there is even now a reporter (the *Federal Appendix*) for "unpublished" decisions.

27. That these unreported decisions may not be cited to Illinois courts or administrative agencies as binding authority does not keep them from being cited in law review footnotes or from being used to fashion arguments that do not cite these decisions. Questions arise in an academic setting as to whether the failure to cite a Rule 23 decision is plagiarism when the rule states that the decision may not be cited for practitioners. As to the effect of Rule 23 decisions on administrative agencies, see James W. Chipman, *The Impact of Rule 23 on Administrative Law: One Agency's Perspective*, 87 Ill. B.J. 428 (1999).

28. *Anastasoff v. U.S.*, 223 F.3d 898 (8th Cir. 2000), *dismissed*, 235 F.3d 1054 (8th Cir. en banc 2000).

29. For more information on issues related to unpublished opinions and Illinois Supreme Court Rule 23, see Michael T. Reagan, *Supreme Court Rule 23: The Terrain of the Debate and a Proposed Revision*, 90 Ill. B.J. 180 (2002).

30. The Illinois Supreme Court has also limited the number of decisions that each district may publish. The First District may publish 750 decisions annually, the Second District may publish 250 decisions annually, and the

find a case that is entirely "on point," yet to be prohibited from even mentioning it to the court. Attorneys who do cite to unpublished opinions have been fined in other jurisdictions.[31]

Rule 23 of the Illinois Supreme Court Rules also allows certain cases to be disposed of by a "summary order" where the appellate court unanimously finds that it lacks jurisdiction, or that the disposition of the case "is clearly controlled by case law precedent, statute, or rules of court."[32] A summary order may also be used where the appeal is moot, where no error of law appears on the record, where the trial court or agency did not abuse its discretion, or where the record does not demonstrate that the decision of the trier of fact is against the manifest weight of the evidence.

C. Circuit Courts

1. Overview

The circuit court is the court of original jurisdiction in Illinois, except for a small number of cases where the Illinois Supreme Court has original and exclusive jurisdiction.[33] This constitutional grant of

---

Third, Fourth, and Fifth Districts may each publish 150 decisions annually. See John Flynn Rooney, *Lawyers Debate What Appeals Court Left Unsaid*, Chicago Daily Law Bulletin, Apr. 27, 2002, at 5. The order limiting the number of publishable opinions also suggested that opinions be no longer than 20 pages, excluding dissents and special concurrences, which are limited to five pages. *See id.* The Illinois Supreme Court has not imposed a similar limit on its own decisions.

31. A colleague in Wisconsin, Christopher Wren, notes that Wisconsin courts have imposed monetary penalties on attorneys who cite unpublished opinions. *See e.g. Tamminen v. Aetna Casualty & Surety Co.*, 327 N.W.2d 55, 67 (Wis. 1982) ($50 penalty); *Hagen v. Gulrud*, 442 N.W.2d 570, 573 (Wis. App. 1989) ($100 penalty); *City of Madison v. Lange*, 408 N.W.2d 763, 765 n.2 (Wis. App. 1987) ($50 penalty).

32. Ill. Sup. Ct. R. 23(c).

33. Ill. Const. art. VI, §9. The cases where the Illinois Supreme Court has original and exclusive jurisdiction relate to legislative redistricting and the ability of the Governor to serve in office.

original jurisdiction to the circuit court was intended to create a single trial court that would have jurisdiction to adjudicate all controversies.[34] But while the circuit courts in Illinois have plenary jurisdiction to adjudicate all controversies, they must wait until the controversies are brought to the court. They can only grant relief that is sought in pleadings (such as complaints) that are filed with the court. A court cannot decide issues *sua sponte* (on its own), nor can the court grant relief that the parties did not ask for in their pleadings.[35]

It is at the circuit court where cases begin, although in some cases the circuit court can act as a reviewing body over decisions reached by certain administrative agencies.

2. Finding Information on the Circuit Courts

Illinois has 22 circuit courts for its 102 counties. Three of the circuits are single county circuits – these are the Circuit Courts of Cook County, Will County, and DuPage County. The other 19 circuits cover multiple counties – from two to twelve, depending on the local population.

Many circuit courts maintain their own websites.[36] The range of information and services differ from site to site. Sites include information about library hours, getting information on specific cases, and obtaining court publications or forms. There may be history about the particular court and information about the judges who serve for each court. Some sites allow you to search for information on specific cases. Clients with traffic tickets can pay fines on some websites. Some sites allow you to sign up for email notices when

---

34. *See e.g. Steinbrecher v. Steinbrecher*, 759 N.E.2d 509, 518 (Ill. 2001).
35. *Ligon v. Williams*, 637 N.E.2d 633, 638 (Ill. App. 1st Dist. 1994) (the court's authority to exercise its jurisdiction and resolve justiciable questions is invoked by filing a complaint or petition); *see also* 735 Ill. Comp. Stat. 5/2-201 (West 2001) ("Every action, unless otherwise expressly provided by statute, shall be commenced by the filing of a complaint.").
36. *See* Appendix A.

something happens in a particular case, or when there are changes to court rules. There may be links to other useful sites. The only way to keep current on the information and various services that each site offers is to visit those sites on a regular basis.

Website addresses for specific courts are subject to change, as is the information available on each site. These sites have changed many aspects of practice at the trial court level, as attorneys no longer need to go to the courthouse to access information about specific cases. Some courts can also be expected to introduce electronic filing of documents in the near future.

3. Appeals from the Circuit Court

If the circuit court acquits a criminal defendant after a trial on the merits, the prosecutor cannot appeal.[37] If the circuit court convicts a criminal defendant and imposes a death sentence upon the defendant, the defendant can appeal that case directly from the circuit court to the Illinois Supreme Court as a matter of right.[38]

All other final judgments in criminal and civil cases entered by the circuit court can be appealed to the appropriate judicial district of the Illinois Appellate Court.[39] A decision from the Cook County Circuit Court, for example, can be appealed to the First Judicial District of the Illinois Appellate Court. The appeal must be filed within the time allowed by statute – failure to file in time means that the appellate court will not hear the case no matter how meritorious the claims may be. The notice of appeal is jurisdictional, and the failure to timely file the notice of appeal deprives the appellate court of jurisdiction.[40] The party appealing must also post a bond.

---

37. Ill. Const. art. VI, §6.
38. Ill. Const. art. VI, §4(b). In some other legal systems, such as in Korea or Japan, the prosecutor can appeal if the defendant is acquitted.
39. *See* Ill. S. Ct. R. 301 ("Every final judgment of a circuit court in a civil case is appealable as of right.").
40. *See e.g. Berg v. Allied Security, Inc.*, 737 N.E.2d 160, 161 (Ill. 2000).

The law generally guarantees each losing side at least one appeal. For example, the Illinois Appellate Court must review the appeal from the circuit court. Further review by the Illinois Supreme Court is, however, discretionary.[41] Under this process of discretionary further review, a party who loses at the appellate court level may file a petition to the Illinois Supreme Court to ask it to review the case. The case will be reviewed by the Illinois Supreme Court only if the court agrees to do so.[42]

4. Researching Circuit Court Decisions

Decisions of the circuit court are no longer published,[43] but "slip opinions" and orders can sometimes be found in the court files for particular cases. Individual circuit court opinions, if they are of particular importance or interest, may be reported in a topical looseleaf reporter.[44] One reason that circuit court opinions are generally not published is because they are not binding on other judges. They are not even binding on the same judge who wrote the decision, unless the later case involves the same parties. (In cases involving the same parties, issues decided in earlier cases are *res judicata* – matters already decided that should not be decided again.)

---

41. There are some limited exceptions when further appeal to the Illinois Supreme Court will be as a matter of right rather than discretion. *See* Ill. Const. art. VI, § 4(c).

42. If the Illinois Supreme Court does hear the appeal, further review to the U.S. Supreme Court will also be discretionary by writ of *certiorari*.

43. True legal research trivia fans will be thrilled to learn that circuit court opinions were published from 1907 to 1909 by Flood and Company. The three-volume set was called *Illinois Circuit Court Reports: Reports of Cases Decided in the Circuit, Superior, Criminal, Probate, County and Municipal Courts in Illinois and Including the Unreported Decisions of the Supreme Court of Illinois*. Roger F. Jacobs, *Judicial System, Court Reports, and Rules of Court*, in *Illinois Legal Research Sourcebook*, at 2–19 (Ill. Inst. for CLE 1977).

44. Jean McKnight, *Researching Illinois Court Opinions*, 85 Ill. B.J. 445, 445 (1997).

If you do need to find a decision from a relatively recent circuit court decision, you can check the court file for that decision. Further information is available from the clerk of the particular circuit court.

5. Researching Civil Jury Verdicts and Settlements

Although decisions from the circuit court are no longer reported, jury verdicts and settlements are frequently summarized in the weekly *Cook County Jury Verdict Reporter* and monthly *Illinois Jury Verdict Reporter*. Regular updates from that reporter are also published in the *Chicago Daily Law Bulletin*.

a. Jury Verdict Reporters

One area of legal research that is often useful (but seldom taught in law school) is the ability to determine the monetary damages that civil juries award in similar cases or that parties negotiate between themselves. This information frequently allows plaintiffs, defendants, and insurance companies to reach comparable settlements more quickly. The reports also indicate the circumstances under which defendants are not held liable for injuries.[45] The information assists trial court judges in ensuring that damage awards are relatively stable while still allowing the flexibility in awards that individual cases may demand.

The *Jury Verdict Reporter* is a publication that began in Illinois in 1959 when newspaper reporter Max Sonderby began to collect, summarize, and publish reports of civil jury verdicts and negotiated settlements. The Law Bulletin Publishing Company, a Chicago-based publisher, purchased the business in 1991 and began to computerize the reports. The company now has a database of more than 45,000 cases.

There is now a weekly *Cook County Jury Verdict Reporter* and a monthly *Illinois Jury Verdict Reporter*. Each jury verdict report con-

---

45. The reports use the criminal law phrase "not guilty" to describe a ruling for a defendant who is found not liable in a civil case.

tains a wealth of useful information for those involved in similar litigation. A report will include:
1. Case Name. The name of the parties involved, court docket numbers, and trial dates.
2. Verdict. The amount awarded by the jury or judge, broken down to identify items such as past medical expenses, future medical expenses, pain and suffering, disfigurement, disability, loss of consortium, loss of society, medical expenses, funeral expenses, counseling costs, lost wages, and other compensatory damages, as well as punitive damage awards and offsets for assumption of risk or contributory negligence.
3. Trial Judge. The name of the presiding judge may offer insights to parties appearing before the same judge. Researchers may also wish to consult a separate publication of judicial biographies, which is updated annually.
4. Plaintiff's Attorney. The report includes the name of individual attorneys, law firms, and cities for the plaintiff's attorney. Also included is the amount of any demand for settlement (labeled as "DEMAND") and the amount that the plaintiff's attorney asks the jury to award (labeled in the report as "ASKED"). The demand and asking amounts should be compared to the amounts actually awarded.
5. Defendant's Attorney. In addition to the names, law firms, and cities of the defense attorneys, the report may include the amounts offered to settle cases (labeled in the reports as "OFFER"). These settlement offers should also be compared to the amounts actually awarded by the judge or jury.
6. Treating Doctors. The report may include the names and specialties of doctors used by the plaintiff or defendant.
7. Other Experts. The report may include the name, address and phone number of experts used by the plaintiff or the defendant. This information is useful in locating an expert or when deposing the same expert.
8. Facts. The report will summarize the facts and contentions of the parties. This summary will show how similar (or

different) a case may be, so that the attorney may compare the amount awarded (or denied, if there was no finding of liability).

In addition to reports of awards and settlements in Illinois, the *Jury Verdict Reporter* also reports information on new Illinois lawsuits in the areas of medical malpractice, attorney malpractice, and product liability.

Jury verdict reports can be researched by reviewing back issues of the published reports or by using the on-line database in the Law Bulletin's "Access Plus" service. The Access Plus Service also includes access to Cook County Circuit Court dockets, building code violations, bankruptcy filings, pending lawsuits, liens, and post-judgment actions. The Law Bulletin Publishing Company can also conduct a customized search for a fee. The results of the customized search can include damage awards or settlements for cases involving similar accidents or injuries, as well as cases involving the same opposing counsel, judge, or expert witnesses.[46]

b. Jury Verdicts and Settlements from Other Jurisdictions

In addition to researching reports of verdicts and settlements in Illinois, attorneys may wish to investigate awards and settlements from other jurisdictions. In searching awards from other jurisdictions, lawyers may find cases with closer factual similarities. Lawyers can search neighboring jurisdictions, such as Missouri[47] or Wisconsin,[48] or they may use the *National Jury Verdict Reporter* published by

---

46. Information about the jury verdict reporters is available from John Kirkton, Law Bulletin Publishing Company, 415 N. State St., Chicago, IL 60610; tel. (312) 644-7800; email: Kirkton@LawBulletin.com; Web page: www.lawbulletin.com

47. The *Verdict Reporter* of St. Louis, Missouri may sometimes also include Illinois cases that are reported to it. Information on its print and electronic publications is available at www.verdictreporter.com.

48. For information about the *Wisconsin Jury Verdict Reporter*, contact 723 S. Main Street, Racine, WI 53403, or call (262) 635-0400.

the National Law Journal.[49] The *National Jury Verdict Reporter* also includes cases from Illinois.

c. Appellate Review of Damages

Lawyers will also be interested in whether damage awards in Illinois are likely to be affirmed, reduced, or vacated on appeal. While this research can be done using conventional case research, it may be faster and more efficient to consult the *Appellate Review of Damages*, a new publication that examines where Illinois cases are affirmed or reduced.[50] The *Appellate Review of Damages* includes appellate docket numbers and decision dates, but there may not be a case citation because the publication may appear before a case is published in the official or unofficial reporters. A clever researcher may, however, find the citation (and the text of the decision) by using the docket number as a search term in an electronic database such as Lexis or Westlaw.

6. Illinois Criminal Justice Information Authority

There are few resources available for those researching criminal cases at the trial court level, as most researchers will be interested in the statutes and the decisions from the Illinois Supreme Court and the Illinois Appellate Court.[51] Useful statistical information and analysis is available, however, from the Illinois Criminal Justice In-

---

49. For more information, contact the National Law Journal Litigation Services Network, 128 Carleton Avenue, East Islip, NY 11730, or call (800) 832-1900. Information about national searches is available from www.VerdictSearch.com. Additionally, the National Association of State Jury Verdict Reporters maintains a website at www.juryverdicts.com. The website includes a searchable database of expert witnesses.

50. If the publication is not available in your law library, you can call the Law Bulletin Publishing Company at (312) 644-4338 for more information or a sample copy.

51. A useful resource for appellate decisions is David P. Bergschneider, *Illinois Handbook of Criminal Law Decisions* (Ill. State Bar Assn. & Office of the State Appellate Defender 1998).

formation Authority, a state agency dedicated to improving the administration of criminal justice in Illinois. The Authority publishes a newsletter *On Good Authority* and other publications on criminal justice research issues in Illinois.[52]

III. Illinois Court of Claims

The State of Illinois cannot be sued in the circuit courts, because exclusive jurisdiction to sue the state rests with the Illinois Court of Claims.[53]

The Illinois General Assembly established a Commission of Claims in 1877.[54] In 1903, the Commission was replaced by the Illinois Court of Claims.[55] As might be expected of any body, its jurisdiction and structure have changed from time to time over the last hundred years.

The Illinois Court of Claims is not a true court, but is better characterized as an administrative agency for the Illinois General Assembly. The court has very limited jurisdiction – it essentially reviews all monetary claims against the State of Illinois and makes recommendations to the legislature as to whether the claims should be paid. Where a party seeks a monetary judgment against the state or money payable from state funds, the proper forum is the Illinois Court of Claims.[56] Under the Illinois Court of Claims Act, the court reviews the following claims:

---

52. Contact the Illinois Criminal Justice Authority at 120 S. Riverside Plaza, Suite 1016, Chicago, IL 60606; tel. (312) 793-8550; www.icjia.state.il.us.

53. Marc C. Loro & Carol C. Kirbach, *Hearings Before Illinois Administrative Agencies,* at 14–17, in *Starting Points: The Fundamentals of Practice in Illinois* (Ill. Inst. for CLE 2001).

54. Roger F. Jacobs, *Judicial System, Court Reports, and Rules of Court,* in *Illinois Legal Research Sourcebook,* at 2–12 (Ill. Inst. for CLE 1977).

55. *Id.*

56. *See e.g. James ex rel. Mims v. Mims*, 738 N.E.2d 213, 215 (Ill. App. 1st Dist. 2000) (circuit court had no subject matter jurisdiction to order the

- Monetary claims made against the state (other than workers' compensation claims, or claims for expenses in civil litigation);[57]
- Claims based on contracts made with the State of Illinois;[58]
- Claims against the state made by persons who were falsely imprisoned and later pardoned by the governor;[59]
- Claims made under the Crime Victims Compensation Act;
- Claims under the Illinois National Guardsman's Compensation Act;[60]
- Tort claims against state bodies, including the Board of Trustees of the University of Illinois, the Board of Trustees of Northern Illinois University, and the Board of Trustees of Southern Illinois University.[61]

A case improperly filed in a circuit court will be dismissed if the Illinois Court of Claims has jurisdiction. The Illinois Court of Claims has exclusive jurisdiction over claims assigned to it, even if those claims appear in a counterclaim.[62]

Judges to the Illinois Court of Claims are attorneys who are nominated to the court by the Governor and confirmed by the Illinois Senate.[63] The Illinois Attorney General represents the State of Illinois in all matters before the court. The Illinois Secretary of State maintains records for the court and a website to assist claimants (and their attorneys!).[64]

Department of Public Aid to refund overpayments of child support previously withheld from a father's wages).

57. 705 Ill. Comp. Stat. 505/8(a) (West 2001).
58. 705 Ill. Comp. Stat. 505/8(b) (West 2001).
59. 705 Ill. Comp. Stat. 505/8(c) (West 2001).
60. James E. Duggan, *The Illinois Court of Claims*, 87 Ill. B.J. 283, 283 (1999) (listing all nine areas of the court's jurisdiction).
61. 705 Ill. Comp. Stat. 505/8(d) (West 2001).
62. *Alden Nursing Center-Lakeland, Inc. v. Patla*, 739 N.E.2d 904, 911 (Ill. App. 1st Dist. 2000), *appeal denied*, 744 N.E.2d 283 (Ill. 2001).
63. 705 Ill. Comp. Stat. 505/1 (West 2001).
64. A website with rules, forms, and recently reported cases is available at www.cyberdriveillinois.com. Further information about the Illinois

Decisions of the Court of Claims are reported in a series called the *Court of Claims Reports*. Publication of these reports began in 1905 with reports from the Court of Claim's predecessor, the Illinois Commission of Claims.[65] Professor James Duggan of Southern Illinois University School of Law advises that these reports are found in many county law libraries, law school libraries, and even some major law firm libraries that "receive the Reports under the condition that they make them available to interested members of the public during normal business hours."[66]

As with other areas of legal research, finding decisions of the Illinois Court of Claims has changed in recent years. The full set of decisions of the court are available on Westlaw, LexisNexis, and through the website for the Illinois Secretary of State.[67] The website also includes the rules of the court and complaint forms. The website also allows individuals to file Illinois Crime Victim Compensation applications over the internet. In the future it is expected that additional files of the Court will be accessible to the public over the internet and that claimants will be able to file all types of cases on line.[68]

Decisions of the Illinois Court of Claims can be Shepardized in the *Shepard's Illinois Citations*.[69]

Court of Claims (including a copy of the applicable rules and statutes) is also available from the court at 630 S. College Street, Springfield, IL 62756, or at 100 W. Randolph Street, Suite 10-400, Chicago, IL 60601. See also Marc C. Loro & Carol C. Kirbach, *Hearings Before Illinois Administrative Agencies,* at 14-17 to 14-20, in *Starting Points: The Fundamentals of Practice in Illinois* (Ill. Inst. for CLE 2001).

65. *See* James E. Duggan, *The Illinois Court of Claims*, 87 Ill. B.J. 283 (1999).

66. *Id.* Professor Duggan's article also lists several helpful resources for further information about practice before the Court of Claims.

67. http://www.sos.state.il.us.

68. Letter from Ellen Schanzle-Haskins, Director and Deputy Clerk of the Illinois Court of Claims, to Mark E. Wojcik (May 29, 2002).

69. Information on using Shepard's can be found in chapter 6.

IV. Federal Courts in Illinois

A. Overview

The U.S. Court of Appeals for the Seventh Circuit hears appeals from the federal district courts that sit in Illinois, Indiana, and Wisconsin. If the case involves a patent law issue, however, the case is appealed to the U.S. Court of Appeals for the Federal Circuit.

There are three federal district courts in Illinois: The Northern District, the Central District, and the Southern District. A guide called *Understanding the Federal Courts* provides a useful general introduction to the federal judicial system and its relationship to the legislative and executive branches of the federal government.[70]

Finally, there are also three federal bankruptcy courts in Illinois, in the Northern, Central, and Southern Districts.[71]

B. Interplay between the State and Federal Courts

1. *Federal Question Jurisdiction and Pendent Jurisdiction*

The federal courts have jurisdiction over cases that involve federal questions, such as the interpretation or application of a federal statute or international treaty.[72] These federal question cases are heard in federal court. "In general, federal courts may decide cases that involve the United States government, the United States consti-

---

70. Copies are available from the Administrative Office of the U.S. Courts, Thurgood Marshall Federal Judiciary Building, Washington, D.C. 20544.
71. Websites for the courts mentioned in this section can be found in Appendix A.
72. 28 U.S.C. § 1331 ("The district courts shall have original jurisdiction of all civil actions arising under the Constitution, laws, or treaties of the United States.").

tution or federal laws, or controversies between states or between the United States and foreign governments."[73]

2. Pendent Jurisdiction

Many cases involve more than one claim, and not all of those claims may involve federal questions. Many "federal question" cases may thus also involve pendent claims under state law. For example, count I of a complaint may allege a violation of the federal civil rights statute, 42 U.S.C. § 1983. Count II of the complaint may allege a common law claim for false imprisonment or battery. Those common law claims would be under Illinois state law rather than federal law. The federal court must decide those counts of the complaint based on Illinois state law.

3. Removal

If a case involving a federal question is filed in Illinois state court, the defendant may "remove" the case to the federal district court.

4. Diversity Jurisdiction

The federal courts also have original jurisdiction over diversity cases, where the parties are from different states and the amount in controversy exceeds $75,000.[74] Under the U.S. Supreme Court's decision in *Erie R.R. v. Tompkins*,[75] a federal court, sitting in diversity, must apply the law of the forum state, including that state's choice of law rules.[76] This means, for example, that the U.S. District Court for the Northern District of Illinois must normally apply Illinois law if the action is based on the court's diversity jurisdiction.

---

73. Administrative Office of the U.S. Courts, *Understanding the Federal Courts* 7 (1999).
74. 28 U.S.C. § 1332.
75. *Erie R.R. Co. v. Tompkins*, 304 U.S. 64 (1938).
76. *Klaxon Co. v. Stentor Electric Mfg. Co.*, 313 U.S. 487, 496 (1941).

Federal courts may thus apply Illinois law in federal question cases with pendent state claims or in diversity cases that they must decide under Illinois law. The federal courts thus cite Illinois state court decisions.

5. Two Views on Applying State Law

Illinois law is clear when the Illinois Supreme Court has ruled on an issue. If there is a controlling decision from the Illinois Supreme Court, the federal court will apply that decision. But if the Illinois Supreme Court has not yet ruled on a particular issue, the federal courts can look to the decisions of the Illinois Appellate Court.

In the federal courts of Illinois there are two different views on how the federal courts should apply "Illinois law" when the Illinois Supreme Court has not ruled on an issue.

In one version, the federal court will adopt "a hypothetical approach that seeks to predict what the highest state court would do with the problem if it were called on to decide the issue," even if it means that they must reject decisions of the Illinois Appellate Court in making that prediction.[77] This is called the "predictive approach."

A second version arises where there is not an Illinois Supreme Court decision, but a decision from the Illinois Appellate Court. Under this approach, the federal district court will adopt the Illinois law of the district where it sits. For example, a case arising in the city of Chicago would be heard by the U.S. District Court for the Northern District of Illinois. Because Chicago is within the geographic boundaries of the First District of the Illinois Appellate Court, the federal district court would look for a decision from the First District of the Illinois Appellate Court (instead of, for example, law from the Third District). Under this view, the federal district court is not predicting what the Illinois Supreme Court will do, but it is

---

77. See e.g, *Systemax, Inc. v. Schoff*, 972 F. Supp. 439, 441 (N.D. Ill. 1997).

applying the Illinois Appellate Court decision as if it were a state trial court judge bound by that precedent.[78]

There is still debate as to which of the two approaches the federal district courts in Illinois should use.

6. State Courts and Federal Precedent

Although the federal courts sitting in diversity must follow and apply Illinois Supreme Court decisions (and, depending on the approach they use, may also follow decisions of the Illinois Appellate Court), the Illinois state courts are not bound by opinions of the federal district courts or the U.S. Court of Appeals for the Seventh Circuit.[79] For example, the Illinois Appellate Court is not bound by a federal court's prediction of how the Illinois Supreme Court would decide an issue. Furthermore, state courts in Illinois "are not required to follow United States Supreme Court precedent unless the result therein is mandated by the Constitution of the United States."[80] An Illinois state court would be bound by the U.S. Supreme Court's construction of an applicable federal statute, however.

Even though a state court may not be bound by a federal court decision, the state court may find the federal decision to be highly persuasive and may follow it for that reason. Decisions of federal courts thus have an "advisory effect upon Illinois courts, and require respect and consideration, but are not binding on Illinois courts."[81]

---

78. *Allstate Ins. Co. v. Westinghouse Elec. Corp.*, 68 F. Supp. 2d 983, 986 (N.D. Ill. 1999).

79. *See e.g. Hendricks v. Victory Memorial Hosp.*, 755 N.E.2d 1013, 1015 (Ill. App. 2d Dist. 2001).

80. *People v. Gillespie*, 557 N.E.2d 894, 897 (Ill. 1990). *But see also Bianchi v. Savino del Bene Intl. Freight Forwarders, Inc.*, 770 N.E.2d 684, 700 (Ill. App. 1st Dist. 2002) ("[W]e are not bound by the Federal Rules of Civil Procedure or by federal decisions other than decisions of the United States Supreme Court.").

81. *Bianchi*, 770 N.E.2d at 700.

V. A Few More Words about Case Reporters

A. Slip Opinions

Court decisions are first published as "slip opinions." These are issued directly by the court, and now may be posted on the court's website.

B. Advance Sheets

Before cases are published in bound volumes, the slip opinions are published in "advance sheets" that come out in advance of the final bound volumes. The advance sheets are paperbound volumes that can be published quickly and inexpensively. They allow the court to publish its decisions more quickly and allow an opportunity to correct errors before publishing the final bound edition. Errors in a decision published in the advance sheet can be found and corrected before they become permanent.

Attorneys should consider subscribing to advance sheets to keep current with the law. Although it may dramatically increase the reading you need to do, keeping current with the cases is one of the best ways to avoid malpractice.

C. Electronic Sources: Cases and Summaries

In addition to being published in printed formats, Illinois court decisions are available on commercial databases such as Westlaw and LexisNexis. Both companies offer free accounts to law students, although many law students can receive passwords only after completing their first semester of legal research.

A recent entrant to the field of electronic legal research is Loislaw. The Loislaw Illinois law library contains court decisions from 1925,

64 • Illinois Legal Research

court rules, Illinois statutes and legislation, provisions of the Illinois administrative code, Illinois jury instructions for criminal and civil cases, and its own cite checking for cases and statutes. The database will no doubt continue to expand and improve. Information is available from www.loislaw.com.

In addition to the commercial sources, Illinois court decisions are available from the official website at http://www.state.il.us/court/.

Several additional services summarize new court decisions:

1. The Illinois State Bar Association publishes summaries for its members with links to the full court decisions. The summaries are usually sent in the morning after the court posts decisions on the Internet, and the notices include links to the full texts of decisions from the Illinois Supreme Court, the Illinois Appellate Court, and the Seventh Circuit.[82]
2. David A. Youck publishes a free summary service for Illinois court decisions, with daily emails and alerts to rule changes.[83] His messages are often personal and friendly.
3. The official state website recently offered a free subscription service for notices of new court opinions.[84]
4. The Administrative Office of the Illinois Courts prepares a summary sheet of recent court opinions.
5. The Office of the State Appellate Defender, a state agency,[85] prepares a monthly Illinois Criminal Law Digest containing

---

82. Information on this service is available at http://www.isba.org/CourtsBull/courtbullsub.html.

83. For more information contact David A. Youck, 909 S. Poplar Street, P.O. Box 95, Onarga, Illinois 60955; tel. (815) 432-6965 or (815) 268-7713; or email dayouck@prairienet.org.

84. Visit the official web page of the Illinois Courts at http://www.state.il.us/court/Opinions/Sub_Ops.htm.

85. *See* 725 Ill. Comp. Stat. 5/105-1 *et seq.* (West 2001)

recent court decisions and death penalty decisions from throughout the country.[86]
6. The Appellate Lawyers Association prepares a summary of recent appellate decisions.[87]
7. Publications such as the *Chicago Lawyer* include summaries of recent cases.

The number of sources that provide summaries of recent cases should indicate the importance of keeping current with new case developments.

VI. Illinois Digests

A. Need for Digests

Case research is difficult because courts issue thousands of opinions each year. The cases are not published according to their subject matter, but in chronological order, as they are decided. Researchers can use electronic databases to search for specific terms. A search by specific terms will often miss important cases, unless the researcher uses the exact terms that the court used in deciding a case. An effective way of searching for these case authorities is by using the digest.

With so many options available for finding Illinois cases electronically, it is frequently forgotten that the digest systems are often a more effective way of doing legal research. This is because research using the digest is conceptual research – researching legal concepts – rather than looking for specific research terms as is often done in many computerized searches.

---

86. For more information, contact the Administrative Office of the State Appellate Defender, P.O. Box 5780, Springfield, IL 62705 or call (217) 782-7203.
87. For more information on the Appellate Lawyers Association, contact the association at 321 S. Plymouth Court, Chicago, IL 60604.

There were two separate digest systems for Illinois law: The *West's Illinois Digest* and the *Callaghan's Digest*. Unfortunately, the *Callaghan's Illinois Digest* recently went out of print.

B. Headnotes

The digest systems are based on headnotes from reported decisions. The reporter of the decision will pick out important parts of the case and summarize them at the beginning of the published opinion. These summaries of points of law are called "headnotes." Although it will be very tempting to cite or quote these headnotes as "the law," you must resist that temptation. Headnotes are summaries that are written by the publisher rather than by the court. They have no precedential value. As one Illinois court stated: "The editorial summary and headnotes...are not words of the author of the opinion and in themselves have no binding authority as precedents."[88] The headnotes are sometimes wrong. In rare instances, they sometimes even flatly contradict what the court has said in the written opinion.

C. Never Quote a Headnote

If you quote a headnote as legal authority, the judge will either laugh at you or embarrass you publicly. Consider this statement from the U.S. Court of Appeals for the Seventh Circuit, when confronted with a brief that cited headnotes as legal authority:

> The case authority Mahmoud did cite comprises nothing more than headnotes, reiterated essentially verbatim from West's Reporter and the United States Code Annotated. That is not authority, rather, it is a publisher's interpretation of what the particular court stated. We cannot view these meager efforts as any sort of attempt to develop a legal argument for reversal. We view them instead as unmistak-

---

88. *People v. Oetgen*, 378 N.E.2d 1355, 1360 (Ill. App. 3d Dist. 1978).

able indicia that the attorney considered the appeal frivolous and invested his resources accordingly.[89]

Instead of quoting a headnote as authority, you should use the headnotes to locate within the opinion the language that you can quote or summarize. When used this way, headnotes are an indispensable research tool. Get the case, read it, and use the language directly from the case (instead of indirectly from the headnote).

D. Organization of the Digest

What makes these headnotes indispensable is that once they are written for publication with the case, they are then organized into categories that researchers can use to locate the legal authority that they need. The West system, for example, organizes headnotes into seven major categories:

1. Persons
2. Property
3. Contracts
4. Torts
5. Crimes
6. Remedies
7. Government

These categories are obviously broad – each contains hundreds of topics and specific legal issues. But you can see even from this list how cases can be categorized under specific headings so that researchers can find similar cases in one place.

The West Digest System uses more than 400 "topics" to categorize the thousands of cases decided each year. A quick sample of the topics included shows that they are more specific than the seven broad categories listed above. They include, for example:

---

89. *Tyson v. Jones & Laughlin Steel Corp.*, 958 F.2d 756, 762–63 (7th Cir. 1992).

Administrative Law and Procedure
Assault and Battery
Attorney and Client
Automobiles
Bail
Bills and Notes
Burglary
Child Custody
Civil Rights
Colleges and Universities
Constitutional Law
Consumer Protection
Damages
Declaratory Judgment
Deeds
Divorce
Easements
Forfeitures
Insurance
Labor Relations
Libel and Slander
Negligence
Pleading
Searches and Seizures
Sentencing and Punishment
Statutes
Workers' Compensation
Zoning and Planning

There are hundreds of other topics. Even so, the topics are still broad and thousands of cases can fall within each topic. For this reason, a further subdivision is made into "key numbers" that identify very specific legal issues. It may not surprise you to learn that many of these key numbers are still too broad, so that they also are further divided into manageable categories.

If you do not have a specific key number, you can use the *Descriptive Word Index* to find one. And as Jean McKnight notes: "It's an index. You know what to do."[90]

You can also use the *West's Illinois Law Finder* to locate key numbers for specific topics. The book is updated annually and can be extremely useful for research purposes. You can identify the key numbers by looking for the entries with tiny keys next to the numbers.

E. Use the Topic and Key Number from an Illinois Case to Find Other Illinois Cases

If you have an Illinois case on point, you can look to the key number by the headnote at the start of the case (if you are using the version published in *Illinois Digest* or the *Northeastern Reporter*). Once you have found a specific topic and key number, you can use the *Illinois Digest* to find other cases that address the same point of law. You may find a case that has facts more similar to the case you are working on, or you may find a case with a different result.

F. Use the Topic and Key Number from a Non-Illinois Case to Find an Illinois Case

The topics and key numbers for the West Digest System are national. This means that you can find an Illinois case on a specific topic even if your only authority is from Texas, for example. In that Texas decision, find the topic and key number for the particular point of law. Then go to the *Illinois Digest*, and look up that topic and key number. You will find an Illinois case similar to the point you found in Texas. This is a wonderful secret of how to use the *Illinois Digest* most effectively.

---

90. Jean McKnight, *Researching Illinois Court Opinions*, 85 Ill. B.J. 445, 446 (1997).

G. The Wojcik Secret for Using the *Illinois Digest* – Five Up, Five Down

One secret in using the digests effectively is to research not only specific key numbers, but also the numbers that are near a specific key number. I suggest going "five up" and "five down" from the key number that you found. This will show you authorities that are also related to your case, but that may approach it in a different way. Many of my former students have used this method to find exactly the case they needed. They used this method after other research methods (the computer) did not give them the legal authority that they needed to find. Having found it so effective when other methods fail, these researchers now use the technique of searching other key numbers much more often (and no longer as a last resort). The digests are an effective research tool that will help you find the authority that you need.

It is true that you can use Westlaw to search headnotes from Illinois cases. This is a great feature of Westlaw, particularly when you may have a unique search term in addition to the key number. But even though this database is a valuable search tool, the print digests allow you to research related concepts in addition to the specific key number. Searching only a particular key number is like doing legal research while wearing blinders – you see only the narrow field in front of you, and you may miss something that was right next to it.

H. Finding a Topic and Key Number to Use in *West's Illinois Digest*

There are several ways of finding a topic and key number. These strategies should form part – but not all – of your overall legal research.

1. Entries in legal encyclopedias such as *Corpus Juris Secundum* may identify a topic and key number for your research.
2. The annotated statutes, such as West's *United States Code Annotated* or the annotated Illinois statutes, often include references to specific topics and key numbers.

3. If you find a case – any reported case – on point, there may be a headnote at the start of that decision that provides you with the topic and key number.
4. You can use the *Descriptive Word Index* of the digest itself to locate topics and key numbers by using terms related to your research. The *Descriptive Word Index* is a separate volume (or volumes) that contains search terms.

When you find your topic and key number, you should use the "research secret" disclosed in the previous section to see if related legal concepts may hold the key to your research problem. You must also "update" your digest research.

I. Updating Your Digest Research

There are three ways to update research that you find in a digest.[91] You should do all three.

1. *Check the Pocket Part.* Unless the digest volume you are using was published this year, there will likely be a pocket part in the back of the book containing cases decided after the main volume was published. When the pocket part outgrows the main volume, it may be published as a separate pamphlet that should normally be found next to the main volume. The pocket part (or separate supplement) is organized in the same way as the main volume. Look for the same topic, and again use the same research secret of seeing if any related concepts will assist you in your research. If you do not find anything on your topic, check to be sure that you are looking in the right place. Ask a reference librarian if you are unsure. But if you find nothing there, it means that no new cases have been decided on that issue.

---

91. For more information on effective use of digests, *see* Amy E. Sloan, *Basic Legal Research: Tools and Strategies* 80–94 (2d ed., Aspen Publishers 2003).

2. *Check the Interim Pamphlets.* Pocket parts are normally published only once a year. Until the next pocket part is published, you should look for an interim pamphlet that will normally update multiple volumes of the digest (and maybe even the entire digest). It will be organized in the same way as the main digest and the pocket parts.
3. *Look in the Advance Sheets.* The digest will normally tell you that it is "Closing with Cases Reported in" a particular volume of a reporter, such as the *North Eastern Reporter, Second Series* or the *Illinois Decisions.* Once you find where the digest stops, go to the volumes and advance sheets for that reporter and check the Key Number Digest under that same topic and key number. You may discover even more recent decisions on the points of law involved in your problem. Each edition of the advance sheets has a set of headnotes that you can search as the most recent digest in print.[92]

Some people may think that this extensive updating is unnecessary. Sometimes it may indeed be unnecessary. But often enough you will find the most current authority on the subject, and the most recent case will necessarily be the current law. You can always take a chance that there will not be anything there, but that is the attitude of a sloppy researcher and a sloppy lawyer.

VII. An Overlooked Research Resource: The Official Index

The West *Illinois Digest* system is not the only summary of Illinois law. The official reporters have their own summaries of important points of law, and these are published in the reports themselves.

---

92. *See* Amy E. Sloan, *Basic Legal Research: Tools and Strategies* 114–20 (2d ed., Aspen Publishers 2003).

Every volume of the *Illinois Reports* and the *Illinois Appellate Court Reports* contains a "Table of Cases Reported" and an index of the headnotes from the cases in that volume.[93] What many researchers do not realize (particularly if they have been using computerized research more than book research) is that every tenth volume in the *Illinois Reports* and the *Illinois Appellate Court Reports* compiles those case names and headnotes into a cumulative list.

The index of headnotes provides a quick, comprehensive, cost-effective, easy-to-read, and easy-to-use tool for finding recent cases. The only reason why more attorneys do not use this incredible resource is that they simply do not know it exists.

If you only read about this index, you are likely to join the ranks of attorneys who have entirely forgotten about this useful research tool. So as you finish reading this chapter, go and find an index volume for the *Illinois Reports*. The volumes with an index should have a special label. Determine what volumes are covered in the index you have selected. Look up a topic such as "attorney fees" or "statutes" and see what you find listed there. All of the cases you find in this index are from the Illinois Supreme Court, and are binding on all lower state courts. You can repeat this easy exercise with index volumes for the *Illinois Appellate Court Reports*. If you do this exercise, you will acquire a useful research skill that is entirely unknown to most other lawyers.

VIII. Sullivan's Judicial Profiles

Sometimes you will want to know more about a particular judge. This may be because you have a case before that judge, or because

---

93. In case you are overwhelmed by the information in this chapter, the *Illinois Reports* and *Illinois Appellate Court Reports* are the two official reporters of Illinois cases. *West's Illinois Digest*, which we discussed previously, deals with the digest system for the unofficial reporters, which are the *North Eastern Reporter, Second Series*, and the *Illinois Decisions*.

you have to introduce the judge at a bar association meeting. The Law Bulletin Publishing Company publishes an annual Illinois Judicial Directory called *Sullivan's Judicial Profiles*. It includes information on all (or almost all) of the federal and state court judges in Illinois, compiled from biographies, independent research, stories published in the *Chicago Daily Law Bulletin* and *Chicago Lawyer*, appellate decisions, and jury verdict reporters. Information includes professional experience, judicial experience, organizations, family, education, civic activities, publications, awards, and much additional information.

IX. Summary

The information in this chapter provides both an introduction to the courts in Illinois and specific research sources that may be unfamiliar to even the most experienced lawyers and researchers. Although many researchers do their case law research exclusively in computerized sources, there are many traditional and focused tools that researchers should not forget.

Additional Resources

Administrative Office of the Illinois Courts, *Annual Report of the Illinois Courts* (2001).

Arnold, Nancy J., Tim Eaton, & Michael T. Reagan, *The Illinois Supreme Court's 2002 Civil Cases: A New Court Settles In*, 91 Ill. B.J. 172 (2003).

Baniewicz, Evelyn G. *2002 Illinois Supreme Court Criminal Cases: Searches, Statutes, and More on Apprendi*, 91 Ill. B.J. 180 (2003).

Baugher, Peter V. *The Northern District of Illinois on the World Wide Web*, 16 CBA Rec. 30 (Jan. 2002).

Bush, Paul M. *Online Availability of Case Information,* Natl. L.J., May 5, 2003, at C6.

Busharis, Barbara J. & Suzanne E. Rowe, *Florida Legal Research: Sources, Process, and Analysis* 11–38 (2d ed., Carolina Academic Press 2002).

Cahan, Richard. *A Court that Shaped America: Chicago's Federal District Court from Abe Lincoln to Abbie Hoffman* (Nw. U. Press 2002).

Duggan, James E. *The Illinois Court of Claims,* 87 Ill. B.J. 283 (1999).

Duggan, James E. *Internet Update: Cases and Illinois Statutes,* 87 Ill. B.J. 501 (1999).

Gallagher, Michael J., Timothy J. Ashe, Richard C. Huettel, & Richard B. Korn, *Jurisdiction of the Subject Matter,* in *Illinois Civil Practice,* vol. 1, ch. 4 (Ill. Inst. for CLE 1997 & Supp. 2000).

Jacobs, Roger F. *Judicial System, Court Reports, and Rules of Court,* in *Illinois Legal Research Sourcebook,* 2-1 to 2-22 (Ill. Inst. for CLE 1977).

Kunz, Christina L., Deborah A. Schmedemann, Matthew P. Downs, & Ann L. Bateson, *The Process of Legal Research,* 111–44 (5th ed., Aspen L. & Bus. 2000).

McKnight, Jean. *Researching Illinois Court Opinions,* 85 Ill. B.J. 445 (1997).

Mersky, Roy M. & Donald J. Dunn, *Fundamentals of Legal Research,* 21–111 (8th ed., Found. Press 2002).

Nolfi, Edward A. & Pamela R. Tepper, *Basic Legal Research and Writing* 52–76 (Glencoe/McMillan/McGraw Hill 1993).

Sloan, Amy E. *Basic Legal Research: Tools and Strategies,* 73–121 (2d ed., Aspen Publishers 2003).

Spiegel, Frank C. *The Illinois Court of Claims: A Study of State Liability* (U. Ill. Press 1962) (volume 50 of *Illinois Studies in the Social Studies*) (Library of Congress No. 62-13217).

Wendt, Laurel. *Illinois Legal Research Manual* 123–65 and 177–203 (Butterworth Legal Publishers 1988).

Wojcik, Mark E. *Introduction to Legal English: An Introduction to Legal Terminology, Reasoning, and Writing in Plain English* 273–90 (2d ed., Intl. L. Inst. 2001).

Chapter 4

Illinois Statutes and Local Ordinances

"No man's life, liberty or property are safe while the Legislature is in session."[1]

I. Overview

Sometimes your research will begin with the statutes. For example, if you have a client who is charged with violating a statute, your first step will be to read the statute. But statutes come into play in many circumstances. As U.S. Supreme Court Justice Antonin Scalia noted, "We live in an age of legislation, and most new law is statutory law."[2]

Statutes are the written laws passed by a legislative body.[3] A statute may command, prohibit, or authorize a certain action. In Illinois, the Illinois General Assembly will pass a bill that will become law unless the Governor vetoes it. The bill, once passed, may

---

1. *Orr v. Edgar*, 698 N.E.2d 560, 573 (Ill. App. 1st Dist. 1998) (Zwick, J., dissenting) (citing *Final Accounting in the Estate of A.B.*, 1 Tucker (N.Y. Surr.) 247, 249 (1866)).

2. Antonin Scalia, *A Matter of Interpretation: Federal Courts and the Law* 13 (Princeton U. Press 1997).

3. *See Black's Law Dictionary* 1420 (Bryan A. Garner ed., 7th ed., West 1999). *Black's Law Dictionary* collects 38 types of statutes under the definition of "statute." Id. at 1420–21.

be called an "act" or a "statute." It may also be referred to as "legislation" or, simply, a "law."

If you know the citation for a statute, you may most effectively begin your research by reading the text of the statute. If you do not know that citation, or if you are entirely unfamiliar with the area of law covered by the statute, you may prefer to read some background material before finding the text of the statute.[4]

Sometimes your research may involve a purely local issue. County and municipal governments enact "ordinances" rather than statutes.[5]

II. Illinois Statutes

A. Session Laws

The *Laws of the State of Illinois* is the official statutory law of Illinois. This set of books contains the complete texts of all acts and joint resolutions from each session of the Illinois General Assembly. It is arranged chronologically; laws are added as they are passed. The set also includes the full text of executive orders and proclamations from the Governor. This is not a place where you could easily go to look up a statute, but rather the session laws before they are codified into the Illinois Compiled Statutes.

B. Illinois Compiled Statutes

The Illinois Compiled Statutes are published in three unofficial versions:

- *Illinois Compiled Statutes* (State Bar Association Edition) (West)
- *West's Smith-Hurd Illinois Compiled Statutes Annotated* (West)

---

4. Secondary sources are discussed in Chapter 7.
5. *See e.g.* Sarah E. Redfield, *Thinking Like a Lawyer* 5 (Carolina Academic Press 2002).

- *Illinois Compiled Statutes Annotated* (LexisNexis)

This is going to surprise some people, but there is no official version of the Illinois Compiled Statutes. There are only these three unofficial versions. The State Bar Association edition is widely believed to be an official version, probably because its name makes it sound as though it should be an official set. They even include a picture of the Governor in the front of the book. But the state bar association in Illinois is a voluntary bar association, and the state bar association edition of the Illinois Compiled Statutes is not an official version.

It is possible to access the Illinois Compiled Statutes through private commercial services such as Westlaw or LexisNexis.[6] It is also possible to access the Illinois Compiled Statutes through the state's website. But even the state's website carries an express disclaimer that it is not the "official" collection of Illinois statutes:

> This site contains provisions of the Illinois Compiled Statutes from databases that were created for the use of the members and staff of the Illinois General Assembly. The provisions have NOT been edited for publication, and are NOT in any sense the "official" text of the Illinois Compiled Statutes as enacted into law. The accuracy of any specific provision originating from this site cannot be assured, and you are urged to consult the official documents or contact legal counsel of your choice. This site should not be cited as an official or authoritative source. Court decisions may affect the interpretation and constitutionality of statutes.

Because there is no official set of the Illinois Compiled Statutes, when you are citing to the Illinois Compiled Statutes there is also no reason to prefer one publisher's set over another publisher's. But when you are using the Illinois Compiled Statutes to do research, you absolutely will want to use one (or both) of the annotated versions. The annotated versions are the easiest for researchers to use,

---

6. These computerized sources give you access to session laws, pending legislation, legislative history, and other research tools. Statutes can also be updated by using Shepard's in LexisNexis or KeyCite in Westlaw.

because they include not only the text of the statutes but also the interpretive case notes, references to legislative history, headnotes of judicial decisions, and references to law review articles and other research materials.

A citation for an Illinois statute will generally look like this[7]:

720 Ill. Comp. Stat. 5/12-7.1

This statute is section 12-7.1 of chapter 5 of title 720 of the Illinois Complied Statutes. Illinois does not use the section symbol "§" commonly found in citations for federal statutes and statutes for other states.

The number "720" is not a volume number, but a chapter number. The numbers following are the parts and sections of the chapters. When you have the printed statutes, look on the spine of the book for the chapter number, and then open the book to find the part and section you want.

Lawyers and judges in Illinois commonly use the abbreviation "ILCS" instead of "Ill. Comp. Stat." In practice, and in reading Illinois cases, you would see the same statute cited as:

720 ILCS 5/12-7.1

At some point you will see citations to the *Illinois Revised Statutes* or "Ill. Rev. Stat." Those statutes are no longer in force and you should not be citing them, except for historical purposes. The current version is the *Illinois Compiled Statutes*.

C. Finding a Statute

If you have a citation for a statute, it is easy to find by looking it up in the printed statutes or online in an electronic database. If you do not have a citation, a statute is still easy to find. Use the subject matter index in the annotated statutes. Looking at the annotated versions of the statutes will also provide you with the cases that interpret and apply that statute, citations to legislative history, and ci-

---

7. Citation examples appear in Chapter 11.

tations to secondary sources and other reference materials that may be helpful to you.

As an alternative to the index for the statutes, you might also try using *West's Illinois Law Finder*. This is an annual publication with subject matter listings across a broad band of legal material. Use the *Illinois Law Finder* to look up a particular subject, and it will give you citations to the relevant state (and federal) statutes, as well as citations to relevant secondary sources published by the West Group. The abbreviation "S.H.A." stands for Smith-Hurd's Annotated Statutes, a series now published by West. You will generally not find that abbreviation in other publications; it is used only in the *Illinois Law Finder*.

Illinois statutes can also be searched electronically on databases such as Westlaw, LexisNexis, and LoisLaw. Some of these services include specialized statutory databases, such as the Annotated Illinois Worker's Compensation Statutes database on Westlaw (ILWC-ST).

D. Spell Check Warning

As long as I have your attention here in the middle of this chapter, if you are writing about a statute, be sure that you are writing about a "statute" rather than a "statue." Use the "find" function on your computer to check for the word "statue" before you turn in your final document.

III. Interpreting Statutes

There is considerable debate as to how courts should construe statutes. On the federal level, U.S. Supreme Court Justice Antonin Scalia identified one treatise that he believes accurately describes "[t]he state of the science of statutory interpretation in American law."[8] That treatise provides:

---

8. Antonin Scalia, *A Matter of Interpretation: Federal Courts and the Law* 14 (Princeton U. Press 1997).

> Do not expect anybody's theory of statutory interpretation...to be an accurate statement of what courts actually do with statutes. The hard truth of the matter is that American courts have no intelligible, generally accepted, and consistently applied theory of statutory interpretation.[9]

When doing research on statutes (and to some extent, administrative regulations), it is important to remember that Illinois courts will often employ various "canons of interpretation." For example, the court will say that the primary purpose of statutory construction is to give effect to the intent of the legislature.[10] The language used in the statute is the "best evidence" or "most reliable indicator" of this legislative intent.[11] Where the language of the statute is clear and unambiguous, the court must give effect to the statute as written, without resorting to other tools of statutory construction.[12] But where the language is ambiguous or unclear, the court may look to extrinsic evidence to determine the intention of the legislature in passing the particular bill.

These (and other) canons of interpretation can be found in many sources. One of the easiest to use is a relatively unknown consolidated index the official reports for the Illinois Supreme Court.[13] These rules are also easily found in the "statutes" section of the *Illinois Digest*.

A. The Debate Over Using Legislative History

The term "legislative history" has been described as "the record made during the legislative process."[14] More specifically, the term

---

9. *Id.* (citing Henry M. Hart & Albert M. Sacks, *The Legal Process* 1169 (William S. Eskridge & Philip P. Frickey eds., 1994).

10. *See e.g. In re Detention of Lieberman*, 776 N.E.2d 218, 223 (Ill. 2002).

11. *See id.*

12. *See e.g. Land. v. Bd. of Educ. Of City of Chicago*, 781 N.E.2d 249, 255 (Ill. 2002).

13. *See e.g.* 190 Ill. 2d (2000).

14. Sarah E. Redfield, *Thinking Like a Lawyer* 146 (Carolina Academic Press 2002).

"legislative history" is used to describe a range of materials that may include statements by members of the legislature in floor debates, statements made by legislators in committee hearings, majority and minority committee reports written to describe the reasons for proposing particular legislation, and it sometimes even describes not the statements of the legislators, but the testimony of witnesses who appear before legislative committees to give their views on particular legislation. "Legislative history" can also refer to the record of votes for a particular bill, or a proposed amendment to it. "Legislative history" may refer to looking at how a particular statute has been treated over the years; for example, how a statute may have been amended after being declared unconstitutional by a court of competent jurisdiction. Moreover, the term "legislative history" may describe the larger context in which some pieces of legislation are created. For example, Illinois was the first state to adopt the Model Penal Code, so much of the "legislative history" for that law can be found not in materials specific to Illinois, but in materials used to draft the Model Penal Code.

A court will normally consult legislative history only when there is some ambiguity or vagueness about the meaning of those "plain words" in the statute. The theory is that if the statute cannot be interpreted by just looking at the words of the statute, then the court should look into what the legislature was thinking about when it wrote those words, and that the court should then write an opinion that gives effect to that legislative intention, assuming that doing so will not lead to an absurd result. It may also be possible to determine "legislative intent" by looking to other documents, such as articles authored by the sponsors or co-sponsors of particular bills.[15]

In recent years there has been tremendous debate in the appropriate uses, if any, of legislative history. Justice Antonin Scalia of the U.S. Supreme Court is widely recognized as the leading critic of the increasing use of legislative history to interpret statutes. He laments

---

15. *See* James E. Duggan, *Illinois Legislative History*, 88 Ill. B.J. 665, 665 (2000).

that "[i]n the past few decades,...we have developed a legal culture in which lawyers routinely—and I do mean routinely—make no distinction between the words in the text of the statute and words in its legislative history."[16] He even tells a story of a brief filed in the U.S. Supreme Court where the lawyer wrote: "Unfortunately, the legislative debates are not helpful. Thus, we turn to the other guidepost in this difficult area, statutory language."[17]

Justice Scalia explicitly "reject[s] intent of the legislature as the proper criterion of the law."[18] Thus, he believes that "legislative history should not be used as an authoritative indication of a statute's meaning."[19] He believes the courts must look to the words in a statute, and not elusive intent of the legislature, which after all is a body comprised of many (and competing) views that would not necessarily agree on how to apply the particular language of a statute to a situation they had not considered when they first passed the statute. As Justice Scalia states:

> with respect to 99.99 percent of the issues of construction reaching the courts, there *is* no legislative intent, so that any clues provided by the legislative history are bound to be false. Those issues almost invariably involve points of relative detail, compared with the major sweep of the statute in question. That a majority of both houses of Congress (never mind the President, if he signed rather than vetoes the bill) entertained *any* view with regard to such issues is utterly beyond belief. For a virtual certainty, the majority was blissfully unaware of the *existence* of the issue, much less had any preference as to how it should be resolved.[20]

---

16. Antonin Scalia, *A Matter of Interpretation: Federal Courts and the Law* 31 (Princeton U. Press 1997).

17. *Id.* at 31; *see Green v. Bock Laundry Machine Co.*, 490 U.S. 504, 530 (1989) (Scalia, J., concurring).

18. Antonin Scalia, *A Matter of Interpretation: Federal Courts and the Law* 31 (Princeton U. Press 1997).

19. *Id.* at 29–30.

20. Antonin Scalia, *A Matter of Interpretation: Federal Courts and the Law* 31 (Princeton U. Press 1997) (emphasis in original).

Illinois Statutes and Local Ordinances • 85

The problems that Justice Scalia describes for legislative history on the federal level further include observations that statements made on the floor of the legislature are often made to a largely empty room,[21] as many have noticed when watching broadcasts of legislative debates on C-SPAN television. This means that legislators did not vote for any particular bill after listening to the floor statements of the bill's sponsor. He also notes that members of the legislative committees that issue committee reports may not have written those reports, and may not even read them.[22] Where the legislative committee reports are not written by or even read by the committee members, their use as support for the proper interpretation of statutory language can be properly questioned.

On the state level, problems with discerning the intention of the Illinois General Assembly by looking at state legislative history may present even greater problems than Justice Scalia describes for federal legislation.

First, although the sources of legislative history on the federal level are relatively accessible and easily searchable,[23] the same is not yet true of state legislative materials. The situation is changing, and rapidly so, with the introduction of legislative materials on the Internet, but for some older materials a search for legislative history on a particular point often comes up dry.

Second, there is not a strong tradition in citing Illinois legislative materials to the courts, perhaps because the legislative history on the state level is thought to be so difficult to discern. Indeed, if you were to ask almost any practicing lawyer in Illinois how to research the

---

21. *See id.*
22. *See id.* (quoting legislative excerpts revealing that no member of the Senate Finance Committee appeared to have written a particular report, and that the Chairman of the Senate Finance Committee admitted that he had not read the report in its entirety).
23. For example, an annotated federal statute will often give a direct citation to provisions in the *U.S. Code Congressional and Administrative News,* where excerpts from relevant committee reports are reprinted and easily found.

legislative history of a particular Illinois statute, they would be hard-pressed to give an answer as to which books or materials would prove most helpful in that task. Additionally, the nature of doing legislative research in Illinois has changed with technological advances that make it possible to track recent bills by using the General Assembly website.

But even with Justice Scalia's criticism of relying upon legislative history as a tool of statutory interpretation, and even with the perceived limitations on using legislative history in Illinois, there are many lawyers and judges who will continue a strong tradition of looking to legislative history for interpreting an Illinois statute.

B. Finding Legislative History

Although there are many compiled legislative histories for federal statutes, there are only a few for Illinois statutes,[24] and even these few are difficult to find. Researchers generally must compile their own legislative histories for Illinois statutes.[25] As James Duggan observes, the phrase "Illinois legislative history" is one that "tends to strike fear in the hearts of law clerks and associates, mainly because of memories of tedious cross-checking of indexes, dusty microfiche rooms, and hours and hours spent researching debate transcripts in small print."[26] But as he also observes, "[l]egislative histories can make a difference"[27] in the outcome of litigation, so it is a task that researchers must be willing to undertake.

1. Check the Annotated Statutes

The first step in compiling a legislative history is to see if someone else already did one. Look at the statute in either of the annotated

---

24. *See* Laurel A. Wendt, *Researching Illinois Legislative Histories – A Practical Guide*, 1982 S. Ill. U. L.J. 601, 603.
25. *See id.* at 603–04.
26. James E. Duggan, *Illinois Legislative History*, 88 Ill. B.J. 665, 665 (2000).
27. *Id.*

versions of the Illinois Compiled Statutes (one is published by West; the other version is published by LexisNexis). Read the annotations to see if someone has already collected the legislative history for that statute. You may see, for example, a citation to a law review article or a court decision that explains the statute's legislative history.

If you do not have access to an annotated version of the Illinois statutes, you can look in the *Shepard's Illinois Citations* for similar references to law review articles and judicial decisions that may describe the legislative history.

If you do find legislative history already compiled, you may nonetheless want to do your own legislative history to see if there is additional information on the legislative intent of a particular bill.

2. Identify the Public Act Number

Using the statutory citation, find the Public Act (P.A.) number near the end of the statute. You will be able to find it regardless of whether you are using the state bar association edition of the Illinois Compiled Statutes, the annotated versions published by West or LexisNexis, or the electronic versions on Westlaw or LexisNexis.

A public act number such as P.A. 87-819 tells you that the bill was passed in the 87th General Assembly.

3. Find the Bill Number

Armed with the Public Act number, go to the *Laws of the State of Illinois,* which is a chronological arrangement of public acts. When you find your public act, you will see the bill number near the beginning of the public act. For example, HB 101 is House Bill 101, referring to a bill that originated in the Illinois House of Representatives. SB 101 is Senate Bill 101, referring to a bill that originated in the Illinois Senate.

4. Find the Indexes to Debates

Under the Illinois Constitution of 1970, each chamber of the Illinois General Assembly must keep a transcript of floor debates. It is in these floor debates that you are most likely to find statements that evidence legislative intent.[28]

The House and Senate each have an index. You will need to look at both of these indexes, because debates on the bill took place in both legislative chambers. The bill number does not change between chambers. For example, you can look up HB 2378 in the House index to locate the House debates; you can also look up SB 2378 in the Senate index to locate Senate debates.

In the indexes for each legislative chamber, you will find dates, legislative days, and page numbers. This is in the information you will need to find the transcribed debates.

5. *Finding the Debates*

A bill has to be read three times. On the first reading, the bill is read into the record and there is usually no debate. The bill is referred to a committee, where it may be killed or may be reported on favorably. Debate starts with the second reading of a bill. There may also be debate on the third reading of a bill

For legislative debates before the Constitution of 1970 took effect, there are no transcribed debates. You may find contemporary newspaper accounts of statements from legislators, but no transcribed debates.

For debates that took place once they were being transcribed, how you do research depends on when the bill was debated.

For legislation enacted before 1982, the index will list "legislative days" or the actual dates of debates. You can find the transcription of debates from a particular legislative day on one or more pieces of

---

28. This is just a theory, of course. One legislator who is now a judge publicly confessed that when he was a member of the legislature, some of the statements that he made on the floor of the legislature were not necessarily the "legislative intent" of the bill, but merely statements that he made to persuade his fellow legislators to vote for the bill.

microfiche, depending on how talkative the legislators were that day. When you then find the correct page numbers for the debate on your bill, you may find statements in support of the legislation, statements condemning it, or statements suggesting amendments to it. Then again, you might not find anything useful at all to you. As stated in the Illinois Legislative History Guide prepared by the University of Illinois College of Law: "Researchers of Illinois legislative intent are cautioned that it may not be possible to locate clear statements in the materials described in this guide because legislators frequently do not explain their intent or understanding in published sources."[29]

For debates after 1982, the index will list the dates when the legislation was debated. You look up those dates, and find the transcribed debates on the pages listed in the index. Once again, there may be more than one piece of microfiche if the legislators had a lot to say that day.

For debates after 1999, you may also be able to find what you need on the website for the Illinois General Assembly.[30] There have been many improvements to the website, and it allows you to track legislation from the 90th, 91st, 92nd, and 93rd sessions of the Illinois General Assembly. The service is quite good because you can search it quickly and by using key words.

If reading the legislative history is not enough for you, you can purchase copies of cassette tapes of floor debates in the House and some House Committee Meetings. Further information is available from the Clerk of the Illinois House of Representatives, at (217) 782-4818.

6. House and Senate Journals

The journals for the Illinois House and Illinois Senate must also be consulted. In these journals you will find the text of bills, the votes taken on them, and any veto messages from the Illinois Governor.

---

29. http://www.law.uiuc.edu/library/home/libguide/Refserv/leghistory.htm.
30. http://www.legis.state.il.us/.

IV. Tracking Current Illinois Legislation

Sometimes you will not be interested in the history of bills already passed, but the status of bills presently under consideration. The General Assembly meets in Springfield for two-year sessions. They are not in session for those full two years, but are generally meeting in Springfield from January to May. Special sessions may be called in addition to these times, such as with November veto sessions to reconsider measures that the governor has not approved. Generally, the legislators will consider "substantive" measures in the first year and consider budgetary matters in the second year. That is only a general rule, however, and the legislature may consider any matter properly before it at any time.

Information on current legislation is most easily obtained from the website for the Illinois General Assembly.[31] Using the bill number of legislation that has been introduced, the General Assembly website allows you to check the text of the bill, the text of any house and senate amendments, the sponsors and co-sponsors of the legislation, actions taken by committees, upcoming committee hearings, and the current status of the bill. You can also see what floor and committee votes have been taken, and from that determine whether the bill will pass. You may even be able to access "real-time" floor debates or the transcripts of floor debates held earlier.

To track current legislation on the General Assembly website, you must, of course, know that a bill has been introduced on a certain subject. The General Assembly website will allow you to search bills by subject matter.

If you need information on current legislation that is not on the website, or not yet on the website, you may be able to contact the Legislative Reference Bureau ("LRB") in Springfield. The LRB is staffed with specialists who follow specific subject matter areas as

---

31. http://www.legis.state.il.us/.

well as general developments during the legislative session. The LRB is the body that usually drafts the specific language of bills for members of the General Assembly, as well as amendments to those bills.

Some bills are amended in dramatic ways, such as by striking the full text of the original bill and replacing it with an entirely different bill. A recent bill on secret compartments in motor vehicles, for example, was amended by striking the full text of the original bill and replacing it with language prohibiting the sale of more than one handgun per month to a person not covered by the list of exceptions. The original subject of the bill remained as a motor vehicle bill, so persons interested in supporting or opposing handgun legislation would likely have missed the amended text if they were unaware of it. There are limits to how bills can be amended in this way, but researchers tracking current legislation must always remember to consult the full text of proposed amendments and not rely merely on short descriptive words that may no longer accurately describe the substance of the bill.

Some bills are introduced as "shell bills," with the full intention of replacing the bill later with a different bill.[32] This may be done when there is a deadline to introduce new bills, and the sponsor does not want to miss out on the opportunity to introduce the bill. The "shell bill" is used as a "placeholder" in the legislative process, and the text of the bill will be deleted and replaced with the new text. There are several theories about using shell bills, including that they are used to hide the true nature of legislation from the public until it is too late to respond to a particular proposal. Often, however, persons who would be affected by the bill are still debating the text of a proposed measure, and using the "shell bill" allows them more time to debate those issues.

Legislative matters can also be discussed directly with members of the General Assembly, including the sponsor of proposed legislation.

---

32. There are different ways of recognizing a shell bill. One common way will make a minor "technical change," such as by substituting "that" for "which." Such changes should be made to improve the generally horrific grammar of Illinois statutes, but they are instead shell bills that will later hold substantive legislation.

There are times when members of the General Assembly actually know what is going on. And if they don't, they can ask a member of their legislative staff and get back to you with the answer you need.

Another tool to track legislation is relatively unknown to legal researchers. The *Capitol Fax* newsletter published by Rich Miller features political analysis of legislation, often including the "real" legislative history of a statute. The informality of the newsletter discourages citation to it as a secondary source of authority, but the information in is often cannot be found elsewhere. Subscription information is available by calling (312) 540-3916 or visiting www.capitolfax.com.

V. Citing Statutes from Other Jurisdictions

Sometimes legislation from another jurisdiction may seem to address directly the problem you are researching before an Illinois court. The Illinois court, however, will usually be unresponsive to the citation of "foreign" legislation that does not exist in Illinois. The Illinois Supreme Court, for example, has stated:

> [D]efendant's reference to another state's statute lacks relevance to this case. Our task is not to rewrite section 115-10 or to determine the best means to accomplish the purpose intended by our legislature in enacting that section. We merely ascertain whether the videotaping procedure was contemplated under our statute, and whether section 115-10 accomplished its purpose in a manner consistent with the [constitutional provision]. [Case citation omitted.] The reference to a foreign statute has no significant bearing on this determination.[33]

---

33. *People v. Bowen*, 699 N.E.2d 577, 582 (Ill. 1998). The reference to a "foreign" statute is not to the statute of another country, but another state.

Instead of citing statutes from other jurisdictions, the courts are likely to be more sympathetic to citations of court decisions from other jurisdictions that interpret statutes that are the same or similar to statutes enacted in Illinois. For example, an Illinois court is likely to look at a court decision from another state interpreting a provision of the Uniform Commercial Code. Although the Illinois court will not be bound by that decision from another jurisdiction, it may prove to be highly persuasive to an Illinois court considering the same issue.

VI. Local Ordinances

Local ordinances are not as widely available as the Illinois statutes, but they certainly can be found. Many local public libraries have the ordinances for the cities where they are located. For example, one of the best places to get the most current edition of the Municipal Code for the City of Chicago is at the Harold Washington Public Library. Copies of ordinances may also be obtained from the city clerks of various municipalities or government units.

The *Shepard's Illinois Citations* includes local ordinances, so you can find judicial interpretations of particular ordinances. If there is no citation to a specific local ordinance, you may find that citations to a similar ordinance of another municipality will be of some value to you. You can use the subject-matter index to ordinances in the *Shepard's Illinois Citations,* and you will amaze everyone in your law office by your amazing research skills in finding a judicial interpretation of a similar ordinance from another part of the state.

Still other ordinances are privately published. For example, there is a separate publication for the *Ordinances for the Forest Preserve District of Cook County, Illinois*.

Additional Resources

Busharis, Barbara J. & Suzanne E. Rowe, *Florida Legal Research: Sources, Process, and Analysis* 39–64 (2d ed., Carolina Academic Press 2002).

Duggan, James E. *Illinois Legislative History,* 88 Ill. B.J. 665 (2000).

Duggan, James E. *Internet Update: Cases and Illinois Statutes,* 87 Ill. B.J. 501 (1999).

Edwards, Richard C. *Researching Legislative History,* 84 Ill. B.J. 209 (1996).

Edwards, Richard C. *Researching Legislative History,* http://www.legis.state.il.us/legislation/research.asp

Johnson, Phill. *Using the 'Net to Research Illinois Legislative History,* 91 Ill. B.J. 147 (2003).

Kasper, Michael J. *Using the Single-Subject Rule to Invalidate Legislation: A Better Approach?,* 87 Ill. B.J. 146 (1999).

McKnight, Jean. *Researching Illinois Statutes,* 85 Ill. B.J. 135 (1997).

McKnight, Jean. *Compiling an Illinois Legislative History,* 85 Ill. B.J. 335 (1997).

Reilly, James M. *Administrative Adjudication Offers First-Class Justice,* 89 Ill. B.J. 147 (2001).

Wendt, Laurel A. *Researching Illinois Legislative Histories – A Practical Guide,* 1982 S. Ill. U. L.J. 601.

Wendt, Laurel. *Illinois Legal Research Manual* 11–78 and 95–121 (Butterworth Legal Publishers 1988).

Chapter 5

Illinois Administrative Law

I. Executive Branch

A. State Constitutional Offices

The federal and state governments are often described as having three branches: judicial, legislative, and executive. On the federal level, the executive branch is made up of the President, his Cabinet, and the federal administrative agencies that administer or "execute" the law. On the state level, the executive branch is made up of the Governor, other state constitutional officers (the Lieutenant Governor, Attorney General, Secretary of State, Comptroller, and Treasurer),[1] and the state administrative agencies.

B. Illinois Attorney General

The Attorney General is the legal officer of the State of Illinois,[2] and the Illinois Constitution makes the Attorney General the sole and exclusive authority to represent the people of the Illinois in any litigation where the state is the real party in interest.[3] Among the At-

---

1. Ill. Const. Art. V, § 1.
2. Ill. Const. Art. V, § 15.
3. *See e.g. Lyons v. Ryan*, 780 N.E.2d 1098 (Ill. 2002); Nancy J. Arnold, Tim Eaton, & Michael T. Reagan, *The Illinois Supreme Court's 2002 Civil Cases: A New Court Settles In*, 91 Ill. B.J. 172, 177 (2003).

torney General's duties is to advise state officers, certain state legislators, and state's attorneys on matters relating to their duties.[4] Formal written opinions of the Illinois Attorney General are an often-overlooked source that frequently provides insights into state administrative law issues.[5] These opinions "can be of significant assistance in solving the day to day problems of government; and, because they often deal with issues which are not litigated, they may become a source of law extending beyond the particular issues or parties involved in the original request" for a formal opinion from the Illinois Attorney General.[6]

Earlier opinions of the Illinois Attorney General were published in bound volumes that included an index organized by subject matter and statutory citations.[7] More recent opinions are available on the website for the Illinois Attorney General.[8] Individuals and institutions can also ask to receive all of the Illinois Attorney General opinions by mail. Researchers are often surprised at the wide variety of issues covered by these opinions.[9]

---

4. The Illinois Attorney General is not authorized to issue opinions to private individuals or entities. In the absence of specific statutory authority, the Illinois Attorney General is also not authorized to provide written opinions for public corporations, municipal corporations, townships, or other local political subdivisions. *Statement of Policy of the Attorney General Relating to Furnishing Written Opinions, Illinois Attorney General's Opinions* v (1991).

5. *See e.g.*, Jean McKnight, *Finding Illinois Attorney General Opinions*, 86 Ill. B.J. 393, 393 (1998).

6. *Foreword, Illinois Attorney General's Opinions* iii (1991).

7. Regular publication seems to have stopped in 1983. A volume published in 1991 included Illinois Attorney General opinions from 1985 to 1991.

8. http://www.ag.state.il.us/opinions/opinions.html. You may also find Illinois Attorney General Opinions in other commercial databases.

9. In 2002, for example, Illinois Attorney General Opinion 02-010 (Sept. 4, 2002) concerned the power of the Illinois Secretary of State on matters relating to issuing a driver's license to a foreign citizen who could not obtain a social security number. *See also* Mark E. Wojcik, *Driving Home Security*, The Globe at 2 (Dec. 2002) (newsletter of the Illinois State Bar Association Section of International Law and Immigration Law). In 2003, for

A formal opinion from the Illinois Attorney General is "superior legal guidance over all other legal opinions" unless that opinion is modified by a subsequent Attorney General Opinion or superseded by a judicial opinion.[10] Even if Illinois Attorney General opinions are not binding on a court, they provide useful insights for advocacy and scholarship, as well as an authoritative interpretation that may be binding on a state administrative agency. The Illinois courts have cited many Attorney General opinions, particularly when the opinion construes an Illinois statute that the court has not previously considered.[11]

Attorney General opinions can be Shepardized in the *Shepard's Illinois Citations.*

II. Administrative Agencies

Administrative agencies are created to administer the law in specific subject matter areas. Agencies exist at the federal, state, and

---

example, Illinois Attorney General Opinion 03-001 (Jan. 7, 2003) advised a State's Attorney in Kane County that township highway commissioners have no inherent authority to provide brush pickup services to persons in unincorporated areas of a township. Illinois Attorney General Opinion 03-002 (Jan. 7, 2003) advised the Chairman of the Illinois Prisoner Review Board that it could not restrict members of the public from attending open meetings except in special circumstances. And Illinois Attorney General Opinion 03-003 advised the Illinois State Treasurer on issues relating to insurance benefit proceeds.

10. Interim Report of the Professional Advisory Board, *A Study of the Role and Operations of the Office of the Attorney General* xviii (May 1, 1984).

11. *See e.g., Bd. of Regents of the Regency Univ. Sys. v. Reynard*, 686 N.E.2d 1222, 1229 (Ill. App. 4th Dist. 1997) (finding support for the court's conclusion in a 1975 Attorney General Opinion); *Roche v. County of Lake*, 562 N.E.2d 1210, 1215 (Ill. App. 2d Dist. 1990) (stating that "the opinions of the Attorney General are not binding on this court, though a well-reasoned opinion is entitled to considerable weight in resolving a question of first impression regarding the construction of an Illinois statute.").

local levels.[12] In Illinois, the Illinois General Assembly creates an administrative agency by enacting an "enabling statute" that describes the nature of the agency, the substantive law that it will administer, and the authority of the agency to promulgate and enforce regulations relating to that specific area of the law.[13] Enabling statutes may also limit the powers that an agency may use to accomplish its goals,[14] and a court may declare invalid any agency action that exceeds the scope of powers that the legislature has delegated to the agency.

Proposed regulations in Illinois are published in the *Illinois Register*, and the notice of a proposed rule will include information on how individuals can comment on the proposal.[15] Under the Illinois Administrative Procedures Act,[16] state agencies may promulgate final regulations after members of the public have an opportunity to comment on the proposed regulations. This open process of creating regulations allows persons who best know how proposed regulations will work (for example, members of industries affected by the regulations) to advise the administrative agency on ways to improve the regulations. The openness of the process also allows any member of the public to comment on regulations as well, even if the comment is just one of support for the proposed regulation. There are

---

12. Local administrative agencies may be created in Illinois under the constitutional "home rule" powers. Examples of local administrative agencies include the Cook County Commission on Human Rights and the City of Chicago Commission on Human Relations.

13. *See e.g,* Amy E. Sloan, *Basic Legal Research: Tools and Strategies* 233 (2d ed., Aspen Publishers 2003).

14. *See* Barbara J. Busharis & Suzanne E. Rowe, *Florida Legal Research: Sources, Process, and Analysis* 71 (2d ed., Carolina Academic Press 2002) ("agencies are created to meet specific goals and are given limited powers to help them accomplish goals").

15. On the federal level, notices of proposed rules are published in the *Federal Register*.

16. 5 Ill. Comp. Stat. 100/1 *et seq.*

some who may dispute that this administrative rulemaking process is indeed an open one, but the process generally works well.

In addition to drafting and promulgating regulations, state and local administrative agencies may also bring enforcement actions either before the agency itself or in state court.[17] A useful guide to hearings before certain Illinois administrative agencies is included in a publication from the Illinois Institute for Continuing Legal Education on *The Fundamentals of Law Practice in Illinois*.[18]

A party that is adversely affected by an agency determination may appeal to a court to reverse that action, but usually only after exhausting all available administrative remedies. When a court reviews an administrative agency's action or decision, it will usually not substitute its judgment for that of the agency, but will look to see that the agency followed the proper procedures and that it reached a decision "within the agency's power, as defined by the enabling statute."[19] The court will also normally defer to the interpretation of a statute by an agency charged with administering that statute.[20] The court will give substantial weight to an agency's interpretation of an ambiguous statute.[21]

In addition to judicial overview of agency actions and decisions, the Illinois General Assembly may exercise its powers to enact a new

---

17. *See e.g.* Busharis & Rowe, *supra* note 14, at 71–72; Christina L. Kunz, Deborah A. Schmedemann, Matthew P. Downs, & Ann L. Bateson, *The Process of Legal Research* 286–87 (5th ed., Aspen L. & Bus. 2000). Depending on the agency's statutory authority, a court action may be brought either initially without any administrative proceedings or only after administrative proceedings before the agency.
18. Marc C. Loro and Carol C. Kirbach, *Hearings Before Illinois Administrative Agencies, in Starting Points: The Fundamentals of Practice in Illinois* (Ill. Inst. for CLE 2001).
19. Busharis & Rowe, *supra* note 14, at 72.
20. *In re County Collector of DuPage County*, 718 N.E.2d 164, 169 (Ill. 1999).
21. *Gem Electronics v. Dept. of Revenue*, 702 N.E.2d 529, 531–32 (Ill. 1998).

law (or amend an existing law) to repeal or alter an agency's decision. The General Assembly may vote to restrict the agency's budget, and it may even decide to abolish the agency altogether.[22] Short of those drastic measures, the General Assembly may hold hearings to review an administrative agency's overall performance.[23]

Administrative agencies fulfill an important role in the overall functioning of government. For many citizens, state agencies are the most important units of government because they are the ones that may most likely affect a citizen's daily affairs.

The Illinois Court of Claims, an administrative agency where individuals can sue the State of Illinois, was previously discussed in Chapter 3.

III. How to Research Administrative Law

There are several goals that a researcher must consider when researching an administrative law issue in Illinois.[24] These goals apply to both federal and state administrative research. They are:

    A. Find the enabling statute;
    B. Find judicial and administrative cases that interpret the enabling statute;
    C. Find agency regulations;
    D. Find judicial and administrative cases that interpret the regulations;
    E. Find secondary sources that interpret the statute and regulations;
    F. Check other official sources for possible additional information; and

---

22. See Busharis & Rowe, *supra* note 14, at 72.
23. See *id.*
24. See *id.* at 73.

G. Check the legislative history of the statute.

An additional goal may be to find secondary sources, such as law review articles, that explain or criticize specific administrative practices, regulations, or decisions. These secondary sources may provide useful insights on how to approach particular research problems.

There will also be times when you want to research the legislative history of a particular statute. Statements made on the floor of the legislature may provide an indication of the legislative intent behind the enactment of a statute.

You may also find that you want to keep track of proposed legislation that may affect an earlier statute. Keeping track of proposed legislation can most easily be done through the website for the Illinois General Assembly.[25]

A. Finding the Enabling Statute

If you have a citation to the agency's enabling statute, look it up in the annotated statutes. Be sure to read all of the sections of the statute so that you have a thorough understanding of the agency's powers and duties, and to be sure that there are no special rules or exceptions that apply to the situation you are researching. Look for statements in the statute itself that may explain the legislature's purpose in creating a particular agency. (If there is a stated purpose, the enabling statute, and decisions taken by the agency, should be construed to promote that stated legislative purpose.) Take care to note dates when statutes (and amendments) entered into effect. You should also look for any statutory periods of limitation that may arise sooner than you expect.

If you do not have a citation to the agency's enabling statute, but you have a citation to the agency's regulations, look at the end of

---

25. http://www.legis.state.il.us.

those regulations to see if there is a reference to the statutory authority for promulgating them.

If you do not have a citation to the statute or regulations, however, you can use the index for the *Illinois Compiled Statutes* to find that citation for the statutes. If you do not know the name of the agency, use general search terms to locate those agencies that may have jurisdiction over the subject matter of your research problem.

You may also find a reference to the enabling statute (or to the regulations, which will lead you to the statute) in a secondary source such as a state legal encyclopedia.[26] You may also find citations in an article in a law review, a bar association journal, or a section newsletter from the Illinois State Bar Association.[27]

Using the Internet, you can find the website for the agency. The agency's website will often contain citations or links to the enabling statute, as well as the agency's own rules and decisions interpreting the statute and rules. Many of these websites are listed in Appendix B.

Many practitioners find that the most helpful research sources are looseleaf services, which are specialized publications that will gather in one place the enabling statute, excerpts from its legislative history, regulations, judicial and administrative decisions interpreting the statute and regulations, and commentary about developments relating to the statute.[28]

If you think there may be some recent changes to the statute, check the *Illinois Legislative Service* to see if any recent legislation af-

---

26. The encyclopedias of Illinois law are *Illinois Law and Practice* and *Illinois Jurisprudence*. These and other secondary sources are discussed further in Chapter 6.

27. The ISBA has many substantive law sections that will review agency actions in particular areas of the law. The ISBA sections publish newsletters that will help keep you current in these substantive areas.

28. These specialized publications (also known as "looseleaf services") are discussed further in Chapter 10.

fects your statute. You can also search the Illinois General Assembly website for legislative proposals that may affect your agency. Even if the proposed legislation did not pass, knowing that legislative changes were proposed (and may again be proposed) may affect the legal advice you give to your clients.

B. Finding Cases that Interpret the Enabling Statute

The annotated statutes are the best source for finding judicial decisions that interpret the agency's enabling statute. After the text of the statute itself, you will find references to all of the cases that have interpreted the statute. You must read the cases summarized there; never rely only on the one-sentence or one-paragraph summary to disclose all of the nuances you need to know about a decision. If your research situation warrants it, you may want to check an annotated version of the repealed *Illinois Revised Statutes* in addition to the annotated versions of the *Illinois Compiled Statutes*.

Another good way of finding judicial decisions that interpret an enabling statute is to Shepardize the statute using the *Shepard's Illinois Citations*. Many people forget that you can Shepardize not only court decisions, but state and federal statutes.

Secondary sources may also provide citations and discussions of particularly important judicial decisions that interpret a statute. This is obviously not a comprehensive search mechanism to find cases, but looking at the secondary sources will help ensure that you do not overlook the most important decisions. You may also find references to court decisions that apply to many agencies rather than just one – which means that you may have missed that important case if you had looked only at the annotated statutes or the *Shepard's* for the statutes.

As a final way of checking that you have all of the judicial decisions interpreting an agency's enabling statute, you can use the citation for the statute as a search term in a computerized search. This may also disclose "unpublished" opinions that you may have otherwise missed.[29] Using the citation as a search term is a technique often forgotten by many researchers.

There may be special reporters for agency decisions. For example, the *Human Rights Reporter for Illinois*, an annual publication, includes cases from the Illinois Human Rights Commission and an index of cases. The *Illinois Public Employee Reporter*, a looseleaf service, includes decisions of the Illinois Labor Relations Board and the Illinois Educational Labor Relations Board.[30]

C. Finding Illinois Regulations

The annotated statutes will often include citations to the administrative regulations promulgated under a particular enabling statute. Illinois regulations are available on CD-ROM and on agency websites.[31]

When you have a citation to Illinois administrative regulations, you should read not only that particular regulation but also all of the related agency regulations to be sure that there are no exceptions or other important provisions that may affect your case.

A judicial decision interpreting a statute may also include citations to the relevant administrative regulations. A secondary source

---

29. Even if you cannot cite an "unpublished" decision to a court, you may find information in an unpublished case that will help you shape your legal analysis and arguments.

30. Information about the *Illinois Public Employee Reporter* is available from LRP Publications, 747 Dresher Road, P.O. Box 980, Horsham, PA 19044; tel. (215) 784-0860.

31. The Weil Publishing Company of Augusta, Maine introduced the Illinois regulations in 2000, but did so by reprinting the 1996 version of the old state-published code and inserted relevant pages from the Illinois Register. *See generally* James E. Duggan, *Illinois Regulations*, 88 Ill. B.J. 417, 418 (2000). This particular print version of the Illinois regulations is difficult to use in its present format because it requires researchers to do their own updating.

(such as a law review article) discussing a statute will often include citations to the agency regulations.

Agency regulations are usually posted on the agency's own website, which may also include references to proposed changes to those regulations. The telephone is another useful tool – many agencies will not only tell you where to find their regulations, they will send you a copy of them as well. They may also send you sample forms, brochures about the agency, and other information that may prove useful to you and your client.

A looseleaf service may include agency regulations in addition to other materials.[32]

Even if you are certain that you have found everything with traditional research tools, you should check the agency's website and the *Illinois Register* to see if any changes are proposed to the agency's regulations. If changes are proposed, you should consider submitting comments on those proposed regulations or attending any hearings that may be held to discuss the proposals.

D. Finding Cases that Interpret the Regulations

Illinois administrative regulations are not annotated. In fact, for many years they were not even being published. There are, however, ways of finding cases that interpret Illinois regulations. Illinois regulations can be Shepardized using the *Shepard's Illinois Citations*. The citation for a particular regulation can also be used as a search term in a computerized search. Depending on the search service you use, you may be able to search both judicial and administrative decisions.

An agency may publish its own decisions, which will usually include citations to the agency's regulations. There may be a special reporter or looseleaf service for a particular agency, or the decisions of an agency may be found on its website or in a commercial database.

---

32. Looseleaf services are discussed in Chapter 10.

E. Finding Secondary Sources that Interpret the Statute or Regulations

Secondary sources may explain, criticize, or praise particular statutes and administrative regulations. These sources can provide useful materials for advocacy and scholarship.[33]

The state encyclopedias include not only a topical index, but also an index of statutory citations. For example, you can use this index to find where your statute is discussed in *Illinois Jurisprudence*.

You should not neglect to search a source such as the *Index to Legal Periodicals* or the *Current Law Index* for relevant law review articles. You may find special symposium issues on Illinois law or other articles specific to your research problem.

IV. Illinois Administrative Law Materials

A. CD Rom, Websites, and Books

Although the Illinois administrative regulations are available in print, they are more easily used from CD-ROM, agency websites, bar association websites, and commercial databases. If you do find a print version of the administrative regulations, you should check for the date when those regulations were published. Do not assume that the regulations are still current.[34]

---

33. Secondary sources are discussed further in Chapter 7, but they are mentioned briefly here because they are often overlooked as sources for research on statutes and regulations.

34. One publisher does have a print version of the Illinois Regulations, which it inexplicably calls the "Code of Illinois Rules." Although the volumes appear to be a current looseleaf version of the Illinois Regulations, it appears to be a reprint of the 1996 regulations, many of which have since

B. Illinois Register

The *Illinois Register* is the official state document for publishing public notices of rulemaking activity by governmental agencies in Illinois. It is published once a week, with a cumulative index published quarterly in March, June, September, and December. This is the official state publication for announcing new regulations and amendments of agency regulations.[35]

The table of contents for the *Illinois Register* will show proposed rules, adopted rules, and other notices that are required to be published. The affected agencies are clearly identified.

C. Historical Research

Your research may not always need to focus on the current law, but what the law was at a particular time in the past. For example, was the action that your client took allowed under the Illinois regulations in 1986? The Illinois administrative regulations were, unfortunately, not regularly published in compiled editions, so doing historical research may prove difficult. If you have been kind to the reference librarians, they may be willing to help you. Whether you can undertake this research depends on whether your law library has these earlier regulations and earlier versions of the *Illinois Register*. Keep in mind that some of this older material may be on microfiche.

If your library does not contain these resources, you may contact the agency directly for copies of those earlier regulations or you may visit the Illinois State Archives in Springfield. The State Archives serves by law as the depository of public records for Illi-

---

been repealed or amended. Researchers must do their own manual updates of the regulations using the *Illinois Register* to obtain a current version of the rule. This updating is a time-consuming and arduous task that the publisher should have done.

35. Recent issues of the *Illinois Register* are also available through the website for the Illinois Secretary of State at http://www.sos.state.il.us/departments/index/register/register.html.

nois state and local governmental agencies that have permanent administrative, legal, or historical research value. The collections in the State Archives do not include manuscript, newspaper, or other nonofficial sources. These Illinois records are made available to the public, officials, and scholars at the Norton Building in Springfield and at seven regional depositories located on state university campuses throughout Illinois. Researchers can also request copies of documents by mail, by fax, by telephone, or by personal visit.[36]

D. Decisions of Administrative Agencies

Unlike some other jurisdictions, there is as of yet no Illinois Administrative Law Reporter to publish important administrative law opinions from the state and local administrative agencies.

Illinois agencies must keep a record of their decisions. The agencies may make these lists (and the decisions) available to attorneys with matters before those agencies. State and local administrative agencies may also publish their decisions and make them available to the public. These decisions are often available on searchable websites.

Additional Resources

Busharis, Barbara J. & Suzanne E. Rowe. *Florida Legal Research: Sources, Process, and Analysis* 71–87 (2d ed., Carolina Academic Press 2002).

Chipman, James W. *The Impact of Rule 23 on Administrative Law: One Agency's Perspective*, 87 Ill. B.J. 428 (1999).

Duggan, James E. *Illinois Regulations*, 88 Ill. B.J. 417 (2000).

---

36. Contact information for the Illinois State Archives is available at http://www.sos.state.il.us/departments/archives/contact1.html.

Duggan, James E. *Researching Illinois Workers' Compensation Law,* 88 Ill. B.J. 291 (2000).

Jacobs, Roger F., *Administrative Law,* in *Illinois Legal Research Sourcebook* 4-1 to 4-19 (Ill. Inst. for CLE 1977).

Kunz, Christina L., Deborah A. Schmedemann, Matthew P. Downs, & Ann L. Bateson. *The Process of Legal Research,* 259–305 (5th ed., Aspen L. & Bus. 2000).

Loro, Marc C. & Carol C. Kirbach, *Hearings Before Illinois Administrative Agencies,* in *Starting Points: The Fundamentals of Practice in Illinois* (Ill. Inst. for CLE 2001).

McKnight, Jean. *Finding Illinois Attorney General Opinions,* 86 Ill. B.J. 393 (1998).

Mersky, Roy M. & Donald J. Dunn. *Fundamentals of Legal Research* 258–94 (8th ed., Foundation Press 2002).

Olmi, Adria P. *Internet Resources for Illinois Corporate and Securities Lawyers,* 90 Ill. B.J. 267 (2002).

Olmi, Adria P. *Treasure Hunting at State Agency Web Sites,* 89 Ill. B.J. 333 (2001).

Price, William A., ed. *Handbook of Illinois Administrative Law* (Ill. State Bar Assn. 2001).

Reilly, James M. *Administrative Adjudication Offers First-Class Justice,* 89 Ill. B.J. 147 (2001).

Sloan, Amy E. *Basic Legal Research: Tools and Strategies,* 233–65 (2d ed., Aspen Publishers 2003).

Wendt, Laurel. *Illinois Legal Research Manual* 79–93 and 167–75 (Butterworth Legal Publishers 1988).

Chapter 6

Updating Primary Authority

I. Why Update Authorities, and What Can Happen If You Don't?

When courts decide cases, they cite earlier court decisions, statutes, and regulations as sources of authority for the decision that they reach. Courts may follow and explain those earlier court decisions, or they may distinguish, question, and even overrule those earlier court decisions.[1] Courts may also declare that a particular statute or regulation is unconstitutional, or find that the particular fact situation presented to the court does not violate the federal or state constitutions.

If your memorandum or brief cites the same authority that a court has previously cited and discussed, you must learn what that court said about the authority you are citing. You must make sure that each authority you are citing is still "good law." This essentially means that you must check to see that the authority you are citing

---

1. The Illinois Supreme Court can overrule decisions of the Illinois Appellate Courts as well as earlier decisions of the Illinois Supreme Court. The Illinois Appellate Courts, however, have no authority to overrule decisions of the Illinois Supreme Court. They may, however, overrule earlier decisions within their own districts.

has not been overruled, vacated, or declared unconstitutional. It also means that you should be sure that other courts are not questioning the authority you are citing. Furthermore, as Professor Amy Sloan notes, "[e]ven if an authority remains valid, the discussion of the authority in later cases can be helpful in your research."[2]

The research tool to determine whether a source is still "good law" is called a "citator." This publication (or online service) collects subsequent citations to the authority you are citing. With information about which cases are still "good law" and which have been overruled or questioned, judges can more easily apply the doctrine of *stare decisis*. Citators also track citations in secondary sources, including legal encyclopedias, A.L.R. Annotations, and law review articles.

The most well known citator is called *Shepard's Citators*, and to use that system is to "Shepardize" an authority. Few Illinois lawyers know that *Shepard's* began in Illinois. In 1873, a 25-year-old man named Frank Shepard was a publisher's representative who called on law offices in Chicago. As he visited these offices, he saw that lawyers were struggling to keep track of legal precedent. He saw that lawyers were writing directly in case reporters when a case was discussed by later courts. Frank Shepard then began his own citator system, which was first a list that lawyers could paste into the case reporters. The list included editorial analysis that showed the impact of the subsequent decision on the precedent it cited. His system of lists eventually developed into a comprehensive research tool to check the precedential value of authorities.

The *Shepard's* system was so reliable that the failure to use it was considered malpractice. Courts have said, for example, that the failure to Shepardize cases relied upon "was not excusable."[3] Another court lamented: "It is obvious that not only was there initial carelessness but the attorney never bothered to check and Shepardize the

---

2. Amy E. Sloan, *Basic Legal Research: Tools and Strategies* 123 (2d ed., Aspen Publishers 2003).

3. *McCarthy v. Oregon Freeze Dry, Inc.*, 976 P.2d 566, 567 (Or. App. 1999).

citations. As a result, it was necessary for the court to waste much time to ferret out the proper citations."[4] Because the court did work the attorney should have done, the court did not look favorably upon that attorney's arguments.

Three examples of additional criticism for an attorney's failure to Shepardize come from federal courts in Illinois. In one case, a judge stated:

> It is really inexcusable for any lawyer to fail, as a matter of routine, to Shepardize all cited cases (a process that has been made much simpler today than it was in the past, given the facility for doing so under Westlaw or LEXIS). Shepardization would of course have revealed that the "precedent" no longer qualified as such.[5]

In an unpublished opinion in another case, a judge wrote:

> Next Khouri...proceeds to cite and quote other decisions of the same vintage by this Court's colleagues Honorable James Zagel and Honorable John Grady to the same effect. But this Court has been aware for the past several years that our Court of Appeals has since ruled otherwise (something that Khouri's lawyers would also have learned if they had only bothered to Shepardize *Gambino*, let alone if they had done a full-fledged proper job of research).[6]

---

4. *Chicken Delight, Inc. v. DeTomasso*, 1970 WL 6952, 1 (N.Y. Sup. Ct. Kings County 1970).
5. *Gosnell v. Rentokil, Inc.*, 175 F.R.D. 508, 510 n.1 (N.D. Ill. 1997). Accord *Fletcher v. Florida*, 858 F. Supp. 169, 172 (M.D. Fla. 1994) (the plaintiffs' failure to Shepardize cases cited resulted in misstatements of the law).
6. *Khouri v. Gies*, 1993 WL 243156, 1 (N.D. Ill. 1993). *See also e.g. Caster v. Hennessey*, 727 F.2d 1075, 1077 (11th Cir. 1984) ("Apparently failing to properly shepardize that case, neither plaintiff's nor defendant's counsel cited to this Court a Florida case, decided after the district court decision here, which specifically rejects *Toussaint*."); *Taylor v. Belger Cartage Service, Inc.*, 102 F.R.D. 172, 180 (W.D. Mo. 1984) (stating that if lawyer had shepardized the case cited, he would have found that later decisions in the Seventh Circuit had restricted the case to its facts).

And in one final example, the court emphasized the importance of Shepardizing by stating, "It is entirely possible to be unaware of a case's subsequent history" because "failure to Shepardize will produce that result"[7] There are many similar examples from other jurisdictions as well.[8]

These judicial pronouncements on the importance of Shepardizing cases show that it is just as important to master the citators as it is to master the primary and secondary sources of law.

II. Using *Shepard's Citators*

Shepard's Citators are available in print, on CD-ROM, and through LexisNexis.[9] Of these various media, the easiest to use is probably through LexisNexis, assuming that the researcher is already otherwise familiar with the basics of using that system.[10] The computerized version is often preferable not only for its ease of use, but because it will frequently include references to older unpublished decisions that may not be found in the print editions.

As suggested in the quote from the federal district court judge in Illinois, it is today much easier to Shepardize cases. *Shepard's Citators* are now available electronically through LexisNexis.[11] Westlaw (which previously used *Shepard's* as well) developed its own system

---

7. *Adamczewski v. Northwest Airlines*, Inc., 530 F. Supp. 100, 103 (N.D. Ill. 1981).
8. *See e.g. Robinson v. City of Philadelphia*, 666 A.2d 1141, 1143 (Pa. Commw. Ct. 1995) ("Shepardizing *Agresta* leads to the discovery that our opinion...states clearly that *Agresta* was overruled by the Supreme Court.").
9. For more information, see www.lexisnexis.com/shepards/.
10. If you need help using LexisNexis, you can contact a law school representative, a reference librarian, or call LexisNexis at (800) 543-6862. If you are a law student (in a semester where you are allowed to use LexisNexis), the number to call for assistance is (800) 45LEXIS.
11. While the CD-ROMS are also easy to use, the online computerized versions may sometimes include more recent cases that are not on particular CD-ROMS.

called "KeyCite." LoisLaw uses its own citator service called "Global-Cite."[12] These computerized systems are taught when learning the basics of LexisNexis and Westlaw, and they are extensively discussed in various national research texts. This chapter assumes that researchers will have some other instruction in using *Shepard's* in addition to the material presented here for Illinois cases.

Although it may be easier to use the electronic version of *Shepard's*, learning the print version is not difficult. There may be times when you do not have access to a computer. Remember, even before *Shepard's* was available online, courts were saying that it was legal malpractice to fail to Shepardize a case. Shepardizing is a skill that you simply must have.

A. Using *Shepard's* in Print to Shepardize Cases

1. Select the Shepard's

There are a number of *Shepard's Citators* for Illinois cases, each with their own coverage areas. You may need to use more than one set of *Shepard's* to be thorough in your research.

Shepard's Illinois Citations allows you to check on citations to Illinois court decisions, the Illinois Constitution, state statutes, court rules, pattern jury instructions, Illinois Attorney General opinions, and local ordinances. The state edition of this Shepard's citator will give you citations from state reports, selected law reviews, and annotations from the *American Law Reports*. It will also give you citations from the lower federal courts and the U.S. Supreme Court.

Shepard's Northeastern Citations include citations for court decisions reported in the *North Eastern Reporter*[13] and other regional re-

---

12. For more information, see www.loislaw.com.
13. The *North Eastern Reporter* includes cases from Illinois, Indiana, Ohio, Massachusetts, and New York. The *Shepard's Northeastern Citations*

porters. This is the citator you would use to find cases from other jurisdictions that cite your particular Illinois authority. The *Shepard's Northeastern Citations* does not include citations to law review articles, so if you want critical commentary on cases you must use the *Shepard's Illinois Citations*.

Federal cases applying Illinois law can be Shepardized using *Shepard's Federal Citations*. Decisions of the U.S. Supreme Court can be Shepardized using *Shepard's United States Citations*.

If all of this is confusing, then you already know why people prefer to Shepardize electronically through LexisNexis. Shepard's publishes more than 200 different citators in print.

2. "What Your Library Should Contain"

After selecting the *Shepard's* that you are going to use, the next step in using *Shepard's* in print is to collect all of the volumes that you will need. To do this, you must find the most recent supplement. This most recent supplement should have been released within the past month or so. The cover of that supplement should include the words "What Your Library Should Contain." Take a few minutes to check that list and be sure that you have all of the volumes and supplements that you will need to check your citation. (If you do not do this step right away, you may forget to do it later. And if you forget to do it later, you may miss a critical citation of your authority.)

If the most recent supplement is more than a month or two old, you should check with the reference librarians to be sure that you have the most recent supplement.

3. Get to Work

Find the right division of the citator. For example, if you are Shepardizing an Illinois Appellate Court decision using the "Ill. App. 3d" citation, be sure you are in that part of the book for the Third

---

tracks citations to cases included in that reporter. Cases that are "unpublished" are not included.

Series of the Illinois Appellate Court reports. You will see the information on the top of the page to let you know you are in the right part of the book.

Once you find the correct division, find the volume number and the page of the case you are Shepardizing. Look over the citations first to find the most current references, and then work backwards from the most recent cases.

Many researchers wonder if they have to look at every case that cites the particular authority. The answer, at least for now, is "yes." Until you understand how to use Shepard's, you should not take the chance of missing a critical citation. Once you have some experience with using the citators, you will know what you must check.

4. Tips for Using Shepard's Effectively

You can Shepardize a published court decision from the Illinois Supreme Court by using the citation from the official *Illinois Reports* or a citation from the unofficial reporters, *North Eastern Reporter* and the *Illinois Decisions*.

You can Shepardize a published court decision from the Illinois Appellate Court by using the citation from the official *Illinois Appellate Court Reports* or a citation from the unofficial reporters, *North Eastern Reporter* and the *Illinois Decisions*.

A good strategy is to start Shepardizing the Illinois Supreme Court and Appellate Court decisions with the official citations, which will give you citations to the Illinois precedent and to any commentary that may discuss your authority. Once you finish that step, you should Shepardize the case again, using the citations from the unofficial *North Eastern Reporter*, which will give you citations of persuasive authority from other jurisdictions.

You should take special care to look at citations with special treatment. For example, a citation with a letter in front of it will indicate something special about the case that warrants your attention. Here is a list of common abbreviations seen with court decisions:

   a   affirmed by a higher court

- c criticized (meaning that the citing opinion disagrees with the result or the reasoning of the case you are citing)
- d distinguished (meaning that the case involves different facts or requires a different rule of law)
- e explained (meaning that the case not only cites the decision, but explains why the previous court reached that decision)
- f followed (the citing opinion treats the case you are Shepardizing as controlling or as persuasive authority that it now adopts)
- j cited in a dissenting opinion
- m modified (on appeal or rehearing, the original decision was changed in some way)
- o overruled (the citing case expressly overrules or disapproves of all or part of the case you are Shepardizing)
- q questioned (the citing case questions whether the case you are Shepardizing is still valid because of some subsequent change in the law, such as a new court decision or an amendment to the statute)
- r reversed by a higher court
- s same case (but usually at a different stage of the litigation)
- v vacated (meaning the opinion has no value as precedent)

You should also note that citations include specific headnote references. You can pinpoint which parts of the opinion are of greatest interest to you.

When you are using the *Shepard's* in print, you may come across citations to court decisions that are not available (or not yet available) in print. If this happens, ask your supervising attorney, law professor, or reference librarian for advice on how to check that authority. The reference may be available electronically if it is not yet available in print.

5. *Daily Update Desk for* Shepard's Citations

You can use *Shepard's* Daily Update Desk Service to learn if your case has been cited since your last supplement arrived. Call 1-800-899-6000 for more information.

B. Shepardizing Statutes and Regulations

Shepardizing statutes and regulations will allow you to determine "the continued enforceability of those authorities."[14] And "[p]erhaps more importantly, these citators direct researchers to cases and secondary authority that construe particular statutory or regulatory provisions."[15]

The citations for statutes and regulations will use these symbols:
- A   Amended (meaning a later law has amended the statute or regulation)
- C   Constitutional (meaning that the statute or regulation has survived a constitutional challenge)
- i   Interpreted (meaning that an authority has interpreted or construed the statute or regulation)
- R   Repealed (meaning that the provision has been repealed or abrogated)
- U   Unconstitutional (meaning that the statute or regulation has been found to violate a provision of the federal or state constitution)
- Va   Valid (meaning that the citing case has upheld the validity of the statute or regulation)
- V   Void (meaning that the citing case has found the statute to be void or invalid)

C. Shepardizing Other Primary Authorities

Researchers can use the *Shepard's Illinois Citations* to find authorities that cite and construe the Illinois Constitutions of 1870 and 1970, decisions of the Illinois Court of Claims, Illinois court rules, and local ordinances.

---

14. Roy M. Mersky & Donald J. Dunn, *Fundamentals of Legal Research* 331 (8th ed., Found. Press 2002).

15. *Id.*

D. Shepardizing Secondary Authority

The Illinois Pattern Jury Instructions can be Shepardized with the *Shepard's Illinois Citations*.

It is possible to Shepardize law review articles using *Shepard's Law Review Citations*. Obviously a law review article cannot be "overruled" – you are looking instead for other primary and secondary authorities that cite an article relevant to your research problem.

III. KeyCite

Westlaw previously used the *Shepard's Citators*. But a few years ago, the West Publishing Company figured out that they could use their own computer databases to achieve a similar citator. The system they developed is called "KeyCite."[16]

Using KeyCite on Westlaw is similar to using *Shepard's* on LexisNexis. Both computerized systems track citations of constitutional provisions, cases, statutes, and regulations. An important difference arises in how each system displays the results of a citation search. *Shepard's* will display results according to the level of authority. For example, subsequent citations by the Illinois Supreme Court will appear before subsequent citations of the same case by the Illinois Appellate Court.

KeyCite will display results according to how extensively a subsequent court discusses a particular decision. For example, a decision from the Illinois Appellate Court that contains an extended discussion of the original case will appear before a decision from the Illinois Supreme Court that only briefly mentions the original case.

Both systems use symbols and colors to indicate the strength or danger of particular citations. You should always remember that no

---

16. For more information, see http://www.westlaw.com/keycite/.

matter what those stars, flags, or circled letters show, you are the one who is ultimately responsible for determining whether a point cited in a case is still good law. For example, you must be the one to decide if the case was "reversed" or "reversed on other grounds" not related to the particular points you are using in your memorandum or brief.

Neither *Shepard's* nor KeyCite can substitute for your own analysis of the effect that subsequent citations have on your authority. But you can use both of those systems to be sure that there are no gaps in coverage between them. If your case is important enough to cite, it is important enough to be sure that it is still "good law." It would be highly embarrassing if an authority you cite is discredited by another case

A wonderful new feature of KeyCite is the "KeyCite Alert." This email service notifies you when there is a change in the status of a case that you want to monitor. This is not a substitute for doing the update work, but it is an easier way of doing it. You can be notified by email of new citations on a daily, weekly, or monthly basis.

IV. Leave to Appeal Table of Cases

The advance sheets for the *Illinois Decisions* contain a list of cases that have been appealed from the Illinois Appellate Court to the Illinois Supreme Court. This list is cumulative, and is published annually in a separate "Leave to Appeal Table of Cases." You should use this list to see if an appellate decision you are citing has been appealed to the Illinois Supreme Court, and if the Illinois Supreme Court has acted on that appeal.

V. Call the Court Clerk

For particularly important cases that were only recently decided by the Illinois Appellate Court, in extreme cases, you may also consider contacting the Appellate Clerk of Court to see if a notice of appeal has been filed for a decision that you are relying upon. You should have the appellate docket number for the case, rather than the page citation of where the case is reported. That docket number appears at the beginning of each case.

VI. Using Sources as Search Terms

If you have access to computerized research services, you can use the name or the citation of a case, statute, regulation, or other authority as a search term in various computerized databases. Doing so may reveal additional citations of your authority. You can also use this method to find, for example, other law review articles written by the same author.

VII. Using Digests to Update Legal Rules

Shepard's and KeyCite allow you to track subsequent citations of specific cases. But when I was a law clerk for a judge on a state supreme court, I learned that courts may adopt rules that would appear to conflict with earlier decisions, even decisions reached within the previous year. Because the court did not want to overrule decisions they had only recently reached, they would announce a new rule without explicit reference to the earlier decision. It thus became important for me not only to Shepardize a specific citation, but to keep track of the ideas underlying that citation. I could do this by using the topic and key number in the state digest.

If you have an important legal point in a case that you are citing, you can look at that case in the *North Eastern Reporter* or the *Illinois Decisions* for a headnote with a topic and key number. Using that topic and key number, you can then look in the *Illinois Digest Second* for later cases that discuss the same important legal point. You should check the bound digest and any pocket part supplements. You should also check the interim cumulative supplements, which you may find in separate pamphlets that are usually kept at the end of the entire digest. These cumulative interim supplements are published more frequently than the annual pocket parts.

Each advance sheet for the *Illinois Decisions* also includes a "mini digest" of points included in that particular issue.[17]

VIII. Chapter Summary

You have an ethical obligation as an officer of the court to be sure that you are citing only the most current law. You also have an obligation to your clients to be sure that your arguments are based on the most current law.

This chapter shows that there are several ways to update authorities. Using any one of these methods should, in theory, lead you to find all of the subsequent references to that authority. But that will not always be the case. You should learn to use all of the different ways of updating authorities, and then use them. Never be surprised when you get to court.

Additional Resources

Busharis, Barbara J. and Suzanne E. Rowe. *Florida Legal Research: Sources, Process, and Analysis* 89–107 (2d ed., Carolina Academic Press 2002).

---

17. *See* Amy E. Sloan, *Basic Legal Research: Tools and Strategies* 114–20 (2d ed., Aspen Publishers 2003).

Kunz, Christina L., Deborah A. Schmedemann, Matthew P. Downs, and Ann L. Bateson. *The Process of Legal Research* 145–62 (5th ed. Aspen L. & Bus. 2000).

Mersky, Roy M. & Donald J. Dunn. *Fundamentals of Legal Research* 312–49 (8th ed., Found. Press 2002).

Sloan, Amy E. *Basic Legal Research: Tools and Strategies* 123–49 (2d ed., Aspen Publishers 2003).

Chapter 7

Secondary Sources

I. Introduction

A. Secondary Sources as a Roadmap

If you are about to drive from Chicago to another city such as DeKalb or Champaign-Urbana, you would most likely look at a roadmap to see the best way to go. The map would show you the most direct route and some indication of the cities and sights you might encounter. It may show you some alternative routes in case you encounter problems along the way. Unless you were already familiar with the best way to reach your destination, or unless you brought along a passenger (co-counsel) who already knew the way, you would be foolish not to look at a map before you began your journey.

Similarly, if you are about to embark upon a legal research journey, your initial time may be best invested by first looking at a secondary source that describes the legal landscape of primary sources.[1]

---

1. Primary sources of law include constitutions, treaties, court decisions, statutes, and administrative regulations. Primary sources may be binding or persuasive (they may be persuasive if they come from another jurisdiction). Secondary sources are never binding. They provide commentary and analysis of the primary authorities, and they may help you understand the primary authorities. They may provide objective analysis of primary sources, or they may criticize primary sources and urge specific reforms.

There are many types of secondary sources, including national and state-specific legal encyclopedias, treatises on particular areas of law, law review and bar journal articles, and continuing education materials or practice guides from organizations such as the Illinois Institute for Continuing Legal Education. Other secondary sources may include restatements, uniform acts, and case annotations in the *American Law Reports*. You can use a guide such as *West's Illinois Law Finder* to locate many different types of secondary sources that are specific to Illinois law. (The only drawback of using the *West's Illinois Law Finder* is that you will only "find" references to secondary sources published by West. You should use the *Illinois Law Finder*, but do not use it to the exclusion of all other sources.)

Secondary sources can provide you with a broad overview of unfamiliar areas of law, citations to leading cases, controlling statutes, and commentary that may help you understand, apply, or distinguish particular legal authorities.

B. Using Secondary Sources to Start and Finish Research

I believe that novice researchers should use secondary sources at two points in their research.

First, if a researcher is approaching an unfamiliar area of law, an appropriate secondary authority can provide the necessary understanding of that area before the researcher looks for particular sources of binding primary authority. Too often law students with free passwords for computerized research services will ignore basic secondary sources and begin searching unfamiliar areas of law by looking immediately for court decisions. These students are essentially trying to complete a jigsaw puzzle by looking for individual pieces before they know what the puzzle is meant to look like, or how big it may be. These students know how to "search," but they have forgotten how to "research."

The second time to consult secondary legal authority is toward the end of your legal research. Looking at a secondary source after you have researched and updated your primary authorities will help to assure you that your research did not stray too far off track, and that you did not overlook any important parts of your research assignment. You will also see nuances that may have eluded your attention when you first started the research project.

Identifying the beginning and end as appropriate points for using secondary sources should not discourage you from consulting them along various midpoints of your research. Just as you can look at a map while you are making the journey, you can glance at the secondary sources to be sure that you are on the right road.

C. Choosing a Secondary Source: Learn about Your Tools

Choosing an appropriate secondary law source is like choosing a tool from a toolbox. You will want to pick the tool that will best serve your needs. The more you know about your tools and what they can do, the better your choice of tool will be.

Using a national legal encyclopedia such as *American Jurisprudence* or *Corpus Juris Secundum* may be like using a globe to get directions for a trip from Chicago to Carbondale, Illinois. You are more likely to need only a map of Illinois. For research problems involving only Illinois law, you may be far better off using a state legal encyclopedia such as *Illinois Jurisprudence* or *Illinois Law and Practice* rather than one of the national encyclopedias.[2]

---

2. The same would be true of using a finding tool such as a digest. The national *Decennial Digest* is likely too large to be useful on a specific question of Illinois law. Instead of using the national or even a regional digest, a researcher will often be much better off using the *Illinois Digest*, which includes decisions from the Illinois Appellate and Supreme Courts, and federal courts that apply Illinois law. A researcher can also limit key number searches to Illinois cases when using Westlaw.

If you are researching an area of law that is entirely unfamiliar to you, you will likely need a source that explains the basics of that area of law, such as a treatise, nutshell, or state-specific legal encyclopedia. When you become somewhat familiar with that area of law, you may benefit from looking at an article in a law review or a bar journal that reviews the most recent developments in the particular practice area.

If you find that the existing Illinois law is adverse to your position, you may want to find a law review article that criticizes the existing Illinois law or that suggests alternatives based on the laws of other jurisdictions.

If you simply need to know how to do some routine matter under the law, you may need a form book with examples of the documents you will need to generate and file.

D. Updating Secondary Sources

Some secondary sources are updated on a regular basis. Some sources are not updated at all, but are written only at a specific moment in time.

Sources that are regularly updated include legal encyclopedias, which may have an annual pocket part, a supplement, new pages for a looseleaf edition, or a revised volume.

Law review articles are examples of secondary sources that are not updated. They are published only as of a particular moment in time, and the law review will normally not publish updates on earlier articles. An article in a publication such as the *Chicago Bar Record* or *Illinois Bar Journal* may sometimes print updates on earlier articles, but those updates are the exception rather than the rule.

Although law review articles are not updated as such, they can be Shepardized by using the *Shepard's Law Review Citations*. The title of a particular article may also be used as a search term in a computerized database of Illinois law, but the failure to find citations to a particular article will not necessarily guarantee that the primary sources cited in an article are still valid. Those primary sources must also be read and updated.

II. Legal Encyclopedias

Legal encyclopedias can be national in scope or specific to Illinois law. How important are state legal encyclopedias for researching Illinois law? Professor James Duggan at Southern Illinois University wrote:

> [F]or state specific issues the savvy researcher needs the scope and coverage of the state legal encyclopedia. These excellent research tools are usually the first place I turn to when doing state legal research.[3]

Because encyclopedias (and Illinois encyclopedias, specifically) are so valuable, they are discussed before any other secondary source in this chapter.

A. Three Functions of Legal Encyclopedias

National and state legal encyclopedias can serve three functions.

1. *Provide an Overview and Background of Unfamiliar Areas.* Just as a general encyclopedia can provide you with a quick overview of a general topic, legal encyclopedias provide a concise and useful overview of an area of law that may be unfamiliar to you. The encyclopedias provide a general text (usually with extensive footnotes to primary sources). The text will give you an overview of a particular subject area, or a particular topic within a subject area. Looking at an overview is like looking at a map before you begin a journey. You will get a good idea of what you will encounter as you conduct your "research journey" through the library, and you will have a good

---

3. James E. Duggan, *Using Illinois Legal Encyclopedias*, 87 Ill. B.J. 167, 167 (1999).

idea about the most direct routes to the research result you want to find. Using a national legal encyclopedia such as *American Jurisprudence* or *Corpus Juris Secundum* can also allow you to see how the rules in your jurisdiction are treated by other jurisdictions. Encyclopedias will not provide you with critical analysis of rules of law or court decisions – for that you should probably consult law review articles – but they will provide you with a basic overview of the controlling rules of law.

2. *Identify Related Legal Issues.* Second, legal encyclopedias can advise you about related areas of law that might otherwise escape your attention. If you are researching a breach of contract case, for example, the encyclopedia entry might remind you to consider whether you may also have a cause of action for tortious interference with contractual relations.

3. *Provide Citations to Primary and Secondary Sources.* Third, legal encyclopedias will provide citations to the leading cases, statutes, and administrative regulations for your research. They will also provide references to key numbers that may be used in the digest system, which will allow you to find cases on specific points covered in the encyclopedia. Because legal encyclopedias are usually updated annually, you should check the pocket parts (or separate pamphlets, if the pocket parts have grown too large) for the most recent citations. Check the date of the pocket part (or pamphlet) to be sure that you have the most current one. You must still update case and statutory citations that you find in those pocket parts or pamphlets.

In addition to providing citations to primary authorities, legal encyclopedias will provide you with citations to secondary authorities that may help your research. These may include other encyclopedias, annotations of cases, form books, practice guides, and important treatises.

Publishers of encyclopedias have historically cited only to other secondary sources that they themselves publish. For example, the *Corpus Juris Secundum* published by the West Group historically cited only to other secondary sources published by the West Group.

Secondary Sources • 131

The *American Jurisprudence* encyclopedia, previously published by the Lawyers' Cooperative Publishing Company, usually cited only to their own publications. Many researchers are unfamiliar with the massive consolidation of legal publishers, however. Now the *Corpus Juris Secundum* and *American Jurisprudence* are both published by the West Group, which is, in turn, owned by the Thomson Company in Canada. This means that both national encyclopedias will eventually cite the same secondary sources. Both of these national legal encyclopedias now also include topics and key numbers that may be used in the *Illinois Digest* to find Illinois cases and federal cases applying Illinois law.[4]

B. State Legal Encyclopedias for Illinois Law

Although national encyclopedias can be helpful to your research, most researchers find that the national encyclopedias (*American Jurisprudence* and *Corpus Juris Secundum*) contain too much information on a particular subject. The national encyclopedias must explain the law in a large number of states and territories, so the entries are necessarily longer than they would be if they focused only on Illinois law. Researchers of Illinois law will usually need a tool that is more directly focused on their needs in Illinois law.

Luckily, there are two state legal encyclopedias specific to Illinois that serve the same three functions as the national encyclopedias. These state encyclopedias provide the background and context of areas of law that may be new or unfamiliar to you; they remind you of related issues you may need to research; and they provide citations to primary sources in Illinois law and secondary sources that you may find helpful in your research. Illinois is also lucky in that two different publishers publish state legal encyclopedias, which means that each encyclopedia will still refer to different secondary sources.

---

4. The digests are not secondary sources as such; they are more in the nature of a finding tool for primary case authority. See Chapter 2 for more information on using the *Illinois Digest*.

The West Group publishes the multi-volume *Illinois Law and Practice,* which James Duggan described as "[t]he matriarch of Illinois legal encyclopedias."[5] The *I.L.P.* will provide references to the two national encyclopedias and to key numbers in the national digest system, which will allow you to find additional cases on a particular point. It will provide citations to Illinois cases and statutes, to case annotations, and to federal cases applying Illinois law. It will provide citations to form books including *American Jurisprudence Pleading and Practice Forms Annotated* and to state-specific books including *Callaghan's Illinois Civil Practice Forms* and *Illinois Forms: Legal and Business.* The *I.L.P.* covers all topics in Illinois law.

Matthew Bender & Company, a member of the LexisNexis Publishing Group, publishes *Illinois Jurisprudence,* an encyclopedia that does not cover all areas of the law but instead focuses on standard subject topics such as contract law, criminal law, and family law.[6] Entries in particular volumes will provide you with useful background information and citations to Illinois cases and statutes, and to federal cases applying Illinois law.[7] Knowledgeable experts are the authors of the various entries. Each chapter refers you to secondary sources including annotations, the *Restatements,* and helpful practice guides specific to Illinois, such as *Callaghan's Illinois Civil Practice Forms* and *Nichols Illinois Civil Practice with Forms.* The *Illinois Jurisprudence* encyclopedia will also refer you to articles in the *Illinois Bar Journal* and law review articles that may provide criticism and analysis of particular rules.

Both state legal encyclopedias, like the national encyclopedias, are updated with annual pocket parts that you should always remember

---

5. James E. Duggan, *Using Illinois Legal Encyclopedias,* 87 Ill. B.J. 167, 167 (1999).

6. *See id.* at 168.

7. The citation format for cases cited in most encyclopedias will not comply with the *ALWD Citation Manual, The Bluebook,* or even local rules of citation. You must take the time to put sources in proper citation format. And just as a reminder, never rely only on the description of the case in the encyclopedia. You must read that case if you are going to cite it.

to consult for the most recent information. (You may find, for example, that a statute discussed in the main volume has been repealed by another statute cited in the pocket part.) Citations to authorities in state legal encyclopedias also tend to be more current than the citations found in national encyclopedias.[8]

In addition to the two state encyclopedias, you may find treatises for specific areas of Illinois law that operate in the same way as the national and state encyclopedias, but provide extensive and specific coverage of a particular area.

C. How to Use the Encyclopedias

1. *Have a Specific Citation to the Encyclopedia, or Use the Index to Find One.* You may find a citation to an encyclopedia entry in a court decision, an annotation, a law review article, or another legal encyclopedia. You might also find an entry when you are updating a case or statute. But in the absence of a citation that leads you to a specific encyclopedia entry, you will have to use the index to locate what you need. You can use the search terms that you developed to find one or more entries in the legal encyclopedias that will assist your research. As with other research, you should keep track of the terms you use and the sources you consult. The indexes will usually lead you to the same place by one of several paths, so keeping track of your research terms and results will make you a more effective researcher.

2. *Table of Cases, and the Table of Statutes.* The encyclopedias can also be used to find ways of explaining particular cases or statutes. The state encyclopedias, *Illinois Jurisprudence* and *Illinois Law and Practice*, have separate index volumes with case names and statutes. You can use these index volumes to find the specific encyclopedia references for any case or statute that you cite in your memoranda, briefs, or articles.

---

8. *See* Amy E. Sloan, *Basic Legal Research: Tools and Strategies* 28 (2d ed., Aspen Publishers 2003).

3. *Digest Key Numbers.* Encyclopedias published by the West Group will include digest key numbers that you can use in a state, regional, or national digest to locate court decisions related to the subject of a particular encyclopedia entry.

D. Citing Encyclopedias as Sources of Authority

Although encyclopedias can provide useful background information, many judges and attorneys strangely do not want to see the national legal encyclopedias cited as authority. The reason for this is unclear, but it may be because national encyclopedias contain too much information (including, for example, both majority and minority rules of law). While you should probably avoid citing to the national encyclopedias when you are practicing law, failing to cite to an encyclopedia that you use in a student work may create plagiarism problems that you should try to avoid. Citing to a state encyclopedia as authority is likely to be more accepted than citing to a national encyclopedia, however, because the state encyclopedias are more likely to reflect the controlling law in the state.

Because encyclopedias are not frequently cited, many researchers forget to use them. They are, however, very useful for researching a new and unfamiliar area of law. They are also useful to consult shortly before you finish your research, so you can again see the "big picture" and be sure that your research was on track.

Specific examples of citing encyclopedias can be found in Chapter 11 (Legal Citations).

III. Treatises

A. Overview

While encyclopedias cover a broad range of topics, a legal treatise is a scholarly book that discusses a particular legal subject in considerable detail. The authors of treatises are lawyers, law professors, or judges who are generally regarded as experts in a particular legal subject. A treatise may be a single volume (such as a hornbook) or it may have multiple volumes. It may be updated by pocket parts, supplements, new pages in a looseleaf publication, or entirely new editions. Some treatises are not updated.

B. Finding a Treatise

You may use library skills that you already possess to find a treatise in a particular subject area. The library card catalog (which, once upon a time, actually did contain index cards) can be searched by subject matter area, title, or keyword. You can ask the reference librarian for assistance in locating a treatise on a specific subject. If your library does not own a particular treatise that you want, ask your reference librarian about obtaining it by inter-library loan.[9] Most treatises are national in scope, but some are specific to Illinois. Here are some examples:

- John E. Corkery, *Illinois Civil and Criminal Evidence* (Law Bulletin Publishing Co. 2000).
- Michael J. Polelle & Bruce L. Ottley, *Illinois Tort Law* (3d ed., LexisNexis 2002).
- Ralph Ruebner, *Illinois Criminal Trial Evidence* (4th ed., Law Bulletin Publishing Co. 2001).

You can find a treatise published by the West Group by using the *Illinois Law Finder*, an annual publication that lists treatises and other sources of Illinois law. The only drawback of this publication is that it cites only those treatises published by the West Group. This is, however, a substantial group of treatises, and you would do yourself a disservice to ignore this source. You may also find a treatise by nontraditional means, such as by looking through a casebook on the sub-

---

9. If you need a source immediately, you may also ask your reference librarian to tell you which other libraries have the volume, and whether you can go to those other libraries to read it.

ject or by browsing through the catalogs of legal publishers. While such searches are hardly comprehensive, you may come across helpful sources that would otherwise escape your attention.[10] Once again, the best help that you can get will be from the reference librarian.

When you are looking for a treatise, you may wonder whether a particular legal book qualifies as a "treatise" or whether it is just another book.[11] The answer may depend on many factors, including the reputation of the authors, the comprehensive nature of a particular work, the reliability of the work, and how courts and other scholars treat the work when they cite to it.

C. Using a Treatise

Treatises can provide you with helpful background on an area of law that is unfamiliar to you. They can provide helpful citations to specific cases, statutes, and other sources of law, and they can provide helpful (or, depending on what they say, unhelpful) commentary about those sources.

You may have a citation to a particular page or section of a treatise. Take time to read not only that section or page, but also other material near it. You will find that the treatise supplies not only citations of primary authority, but also analysis and commentary of the sources cited.[12]

---

10. Information about the catalog for Carolina Academic Press can be found at www.cap-press.com.

11. *See e.g.* Barbara J. Busharis and Suzanne E. Rowe, *Florida Legal Research* 135 (2d ed., Carolina Academic Press 2003) ("Almost any legal text could be called a treatise.").

12. *See e.g.* Christina L. Kunz, Deborah A. Schmedemann, Matthew P. Downs, and Ann L. Bateson, *The Process of Legal Research* 61 (5th ed., Aspen L. & Bus. 2000) ("Most legal treatises provide a fairly comprehensive and scholarly overview of the subject addressed. Because the coverage is typically analytical as well as descriptive, a treatise is often an ideal place to start your research if you are unfamiliar with the subject of your research problem.").

You should always check the table of contents and index of a treatise to locate topics of particular interest to your research. You should look at the table of contents and index even if you already have a citation to a specific page or section.

Some treatises are available online or on CD-ROM. Although such access is useful for searching for specific words or citations within the treatise, you are often better off using the paper version of a treatise. The reason for this is found in the principle of "next-to-it-tiveness." First, when you go to a library shelf to get a treatise, you will see the titles of related works that are "next to it." Second, when you are reading a particular section of a treatise, you will see the related sections that are "next to it." If you do the same research electronically, you will miss the additional sources and closely related alternative theories that you might have used successfully in your research.

D. When Should You Cite a Treatise?

You may wonder whether you should cite a treatise (or other secondary source) in your memoranda, brief, or scholarly article.

If you are a law student and you are writing something for law school, the failure to cite a treatise that you consulted may create serious plagiarism problems. In some cases, the failure to cite a source has prevented students from passing a course, graduating from law school, or being certified to take the bar examination. As a matter of academic honor, you simply must cite the source of any language or idea that you use. You must cite the source even if you put the idea "in your own words." The same is true of practitioners and other authors of law review articles.

If you are a practitioner writing for a court, however, there are different concerns that apply. Judges are generally not as concerned about the academic plagiarism that concerns law school professors. They are concerned with the primary authority that controls the outcome of a case, and you should cite any primary authority that you find, including cases, statutes, and regulations.[13] Nevertheless, you should still consider citing a treatise as secondary authority, particularly if other courts have cited the treatise as being authoritative.[14]

Examples of citation formats for treatises can be found in Chapter 11 (Legal Citations).

IV. Law Review Articles

A. Understanding Legal Periodicals

Law professors, judges, practitioners, and politicians may write law review and bar journal articles. These articles may describe recent developments in specific areas of the law, or they may describe areas of the law that are not yet developed.[15] These law review and bar journal articles may provide citations to binding and persuasive authority, useful criticism of legal rules, and analysis or explanations of public policies that support (or undermine) particular legal rules.[16] Law students may also write comments and casenotes for publication. Comments are similar to other lead articles; casenotes generally describe only a single case and offer some insights into that case.

---

13. *See* Christina L. Kunz, Deborah A. Schmedemann, Matthew P. Downs, and Ann L. Bateson, *The Process of Legal Research* 107 (5th ed., Aspen L. & Bus. 2000).

14. In some instances, it may be appropriate to tell the court that other courts have cited a particular treatise for a specific point of law, even if those other courts are not in Illinois.

15. *See e.g.* Amy E. Sloan, *Basic Legal Research: Tools and Strategies* 32 (2d ed., Aspen Publishers 2003) (Law review articles "can be useful for obtaining an overview of an area of law, finding references to primary and secondary authority, and developing ideas for analyzing a question of first impression or resolving a conflict in the law.").

16. *See e.g.* Christina L. Kunz, Deborah A. Schmedemann, Matthew P. Downs, and Ann L. Bateson, *The Process of Legal Research* 68 (5th ed., Aspen L. & Bus. 2000) (Law review articles "not only describe the current state of the law but also generally explore underlying policies, critique current legal rules, and advocate law reform.").

Law review articles may be used as sources to find primary sources of law and to understand those sources. They may also be used as sources of persuasive authority to convince courts to adopt new rules of law. And as Jean McKnight correctly observes: "Periodicals are among the most important secondary sources for researchers, particularly for rapidly changing areas of the law."[17]

Law is, strangely, the only professional field where students are the primary (and sometimes only) editors of articles. In medical journals, for example, articles are sent for anonymous peer review before they are published. The review helps guarantee the quality of the articles and protects the reputation of the journal. This process of outside review usually does not happen with law review articles, however, or at least those law reviews published by law schools.[18]

In addition to purely academic publications, there are bar association journals and newsletters that contain practical, focused articles on topics encountered in law practice.[19]

B. Finding Law Review Articles and Bar Association Journals

There are thousands of law review articles published each year by hundreds of different law reviews.[20] If your practice involves Illinois

---

17. Jean McKnight, *Researching Illinois Law in Periodicals*, 86 Ill. B.J. 279, 279 (1998).

18. The reason why law review articles are not vetted with other legal professionals is not entirely clear, but there is no prohibition on doing so. If you were writing a law review article, you would indeed be wise to send it to other knowledgeable professionals for their comments on it before it is published. Articles in other law reviews, such as professional publications from the various sections of the American Bar Association, may be reviewed by other legal professionals who are knowledgeable about the issues discussed.

19. *See e.g.* James E. Duggan, *Illinois Bar Association Journals and Newsletters*, 88 Ill. B.J. 175 (2000).

20. *See* Amy E. Sloan, *Basic Legal Research: Tools and Strategies* 35 (2d ed., Aspen Publishers 2003).

law, you might even consider subscribing to one or more of the law reviews and law journals published by law schools in Illinois.[21] The annual subscription cost for these law reviews is extremely reasonable, and you will not have to waste time downloading articles that you already have in your library. You will also keep current with the legal literature, which could be helpful if the judge you are going to argue before has just written a law review article on that subject.

But even if you subscribe to all of the law reviews in Illinois, you will still need an index to find law review articles that may help your research and advocacy. It is possible to search electronically for law review articles using the commercial databases such as Lexis and Westlaw.

There are three print indexes in which you can search for legal periodicals.

The two used for U.S. sources are the *Index to Legal Periodicals and Books* and the *Current Law Index*. These publications do not have identical coverage, but there is substantial overlap in what they do cover. They also may use different search terms to categorize the subject matter of specific law review articles.

The subject and author index for the *Index to Legal Periodicals* and the subject index for the *Current Law Index* are both easy to use. Use your list of search terms to find articles that you need.[22]

A third print index for legal periodicals, the *Index to Foreign Legal Periodicals*, covers law review articles from journals outside the United States. Although you may not need this for a research project

---

21. You can, for example, subscribe to the law reviews published at Chicago-Kent College of Law, the University of Chicago Law School, DePaul University College of Law, the University of Illinois College of Law, The John Marshall Law School, Loyola University of Chicago Law School, Northern Illinois University College of Law, Northwestern University Law School, and Southern Illinois University College of Law.

22. Example pages of both publications are reproduced in Amy E. Sloan, *Basic Legal Research: Tools and Strategies* 36–37 (2d ed., Aspen Publishers 2003).

on Illinois law, it is a useful source to know about when you want sources from outside the United States, or if you are dealing with an international law matter that involves clients or property in Illinois. The subject index is easy to use. The reference librarian can help you locate journals that may not be held in your library.

An electronic index service for legal publications is LegalTrac, which provides indexing for major law reviews, legal newspapers, bar association journals, and international journals.[23]

The full text of many important law review and bar journal articles can also be searched in the databases for LexisNexis and Westlaw. These databases are particularly helpful when the law review article you need is not in your law library. Many students with free access to these computerized services develop a bad habit of printing out all law review articles, however, including those that may be sitting on the library shelves just a few feet away.

Another method of searching law review articles is the HeinOnline service that is now available in many law firms and law libraries. The service provides an image-based searchable database that allows researchers not only to find relevant law review articles, but also to see them exactly as they first appeared in print. This is an advantage for law review articles that include tables and graphs, but it is also comforting to see the familiar law review article format so easily available. Shannon Hein of William S. Hein & Co., Inc., the publisher of HeinOnline, tells me that the company intends to include "every page of every issue of every bound volume, from volume 1 through the most current volume published." The database is indeed constantly expanding. The page images are clear and the service allows law libraries to recover shelf space from older journals. The electronic database allows researchers access to many journals that might otherwise be unavailable.[24]

---

23. Information about subscribing to LegalTrac is available by calling 1-800-877-4253 or at www.gale.com.
24. Journals from Illinois include the *Chicago Journal of International Law* [2000–2002], the *Chicago Law Times* [1887–1889], the *DePaul LCA Journal of Art and Entertainment Law* [1991–2001], the *Illinois Law Quarterly*

A researcher can also find a law review article by coming across a citation to an article while reading something else, such as a judicial decision, encyclopedia entry, or another law review article. This is research by happenstance, but if what you were reading was related to the subject of your legal research project, you should take a moment to inspect the citation you came across. There may be information in that article to help you.

Researchers may Shepardize a judicial decision and learn that the decision has been cited in a law review article.[25] The entry in the *Shepard's* citator will show the exact page that the case is cited on, so it will not take long for a researcher to look at that law review article and determine whether its substance applies to the legal research project.

Because law review articles contain extensive footnotes with citations to primary authority and other secondary authorities, they are useful places to begin research. Law review articles often advocate specific viewpoints on the law, so you will want to be aware of potential biases on the part of the author. Do not feel that you must read all of the law review articles you find; if you are still relatively early in the research process it may be sufficient to skim the articles for a general overview of the article and specific citations to legal authorities.[26]

[1917–1924], the *John Marshall Law Quarterly* [1935–1943], the *Northwestern Law Review* [1893–1896], the *Northwestern University Law Review* [1906–2001], the *Northwestern Journal of International Law and Business* [1979–2001], the *University of Chicago Law Review* [1933–2001] and the *University of Chicago Roundtable* [1993–2001]. Journals to be added include the *Chicago Bar Record*, the *DePaul Business and Commercial Law Journal*, the *DePaul Business Law Journal*, the *DePaul Journal of Health Care Law*, *The John Marshall Law Review*, the *Loyola University of Chicago Law Journal*, the *Northern Illinois University Law Review*, and the *Southern Illinois University Law Review*. Information about the HeinOnline service is available at http://heinonline.com or from Shannon Hein, 1285 Main Street, Buffalo, New York 14209, tel. (800) 828-7571 or s_hein@wshein.com.

25. Use of the *Shepard's Citators* is discussed in Chapter 6.

26. *See* Barbara J. Busharis and Suzanne E. Rowe, *Florida Legal Research: Sources, Process, and Analysis* 129, 132 (2d ed., Carolina Academic Press 2003).

C. Citing Law Review Articles as Authority

Whether to cite a law review article depends on your audience and the nature of the article itself. If you are a law student doing academic work, you must cite the source of all ideas and words to avoid plagiarism problems that may ruin your career. You must also cite these articles if you are a practitioner or legal scholar writing a law review article.[27] But if you are writing a brief for a court, whether you cite the article will depend on a variety of factors, including the reputation of the author, the quality of legal analysis in the article, and the specific suggestions made in the article (including suggestions that may hurt your client's case).[28]

Law review articles can be Shepardized in the *Shepard's Law Review Citations*.

V. Continuing Legal Education Materials

Although continuing legal education is not yet required for lawyers licensed in Illinois, a number of bar associations regularly offer continuing legal education (CLE) programs with excellent materials. The Illinois State Bar Association[29] and Chicago Bar Association are among the groups that hold CLE programs. The Chicago Bar Association Bookstore also sells CLE materials produced by the Illinois Institute for Continuing Legal Education (IICLE).[30] Other groups with CLE materials for Illinois law include the National Busi-

---

27. It is widely expected that law review articles should cite other law review articles, at least as a matter of professional academic courtesy.
28. You may also know something about your reader specifically, such as whether they would welcome citations to law review articles in things written for them. For example, a judge who is a prolific author may welcome citations to law review articles.
29. Further information on current titles is available at www.isba.org.
30. Information about current CLE publications and upcoming courses is available at www.iicle.com.

ness Institute[31] and its subsidiary, the Institute for Paralegal Education.[32] CLE programs and materials are also available from Lorman Educational Services.[33]

Although a lawyer would seldom (if ever) cite CLE materials as legal authority,[34] CLE materials often include extremely helpful research materials and forms that are oriented toward specific practice needs.

VI. Other Secondary Law Sources

Other secondary law sources are not less important than the sources already discussed in this chapter. They are not discussed extensively here, however, because this book is a supplement to the national research texts that you may use. The descriptions here are only a reminder of what you have learned from those other books.

---

31. Recent Illinois titles from the National Business Institute include: James M. Dash & Margery Newman, *Advanced Construction Law in Illinois* (2002); Steven D. Draper & Philip C. Kaufmann, *Computer Assisted Legal Research for Illinois Paralegals* (2002); Jeffrey W. Brend & Carlton R. Marcyan, *Equitable Distribution and Divorce Settlements in Illinois: Valuation, Tax, and Other Issues* (2002); Nancy L. Hirsch, *How to Litigate Your First Civil Trial in Illinois* (2002); Francis A. Spina & Thomas M. Wilde, *Selecting and Terminating Employees in Illinois* (2002); and Laura Manzi & Brooke R. Whitted, *Illinois Special Education Law* (2002). For more information on institute publications, visit www.nbi-sems.com.
32. Recent titles for paralegals in Illinois include Joseph A. Leonardi & Stephen Lesavich, *Internet Strategies for the Paralegal in Illinois* (2002); Eugene K. Hollander & Thomas M. Wilde, *Employment Discrimination Law Update in Illinois* (2002); and Richard S. Kuhlman, *Advanced Personal Injury Practice in Illinois* (2002).
33. www.lorman.com. The website allows you to search for legal publications specific to Illinois. Past programs include Mark E. Wojcik & Howard S. Suskin, *An Effective Approach to Legal Writing and Research* (2001).
34. There are exceptions to every rule. I can imagine citing CLE materials if the judges I am arguing before were the authors of those materials.

Secondary Sources • 145

A. Dictionaries

Legal dictionaries, such as *Ballentine's* or *Black's Law Dictionary* are often consulted as a research resource. Their definitions are sometimes cited by attorneys and courts as a way of explaining words from particular rules of law.

An overlooked dictionary is the publication *Words and Phrases*, which includes definitions from federal and state court decisions. It is possible to use this neglected tool to find the "Illinois definition" of particular terms. *Word and Phrases* is not a resource that you would ever cite as authority. You must cite the cases that you find by using *Words and Phrases*. It should go without saying that you must read those cases before you cite them, and you must also update them to be sure that they are still good law.

Regular dictionaries may also provide you with information that you need. If a word from a statute is to be given its "plain meaning," for example, a regular dictionary may provide that for you.

There will also be special technical dictionaries that may help you, such as a dictionary of computer terms or business practices.

B. Restatements (Annotated)

Restatements say what the law is – or what it ought to be, in the opinion of the law professors, jurists, and practitioners who draft the various restatements for the American Law Institute. The restatements are not binding, but may be adopted by courts as persuasive authority. Once the court adopts a provision from a restatement, that provision then becomes binding (because the court adopted it, and others must now follow the court decision).

The annotated restatements can be used as a research tool. These volumes collect all of the major case citations that apply or interpret each section of each restatement. For example, a researcher may be interested in sections 402A or 402B of the *Restatement (Second) of Torts*, or in a provision from the new *Restatement (Third) of Products*

Liability. A person can use the annotated restatements to find – in one place – descriptions of all of the federal and state cases that have cited a particular provision from a restatement. It is a very useful yet largely unknown research tool.

Restatement sections can also be Shepardized to see where they have been discussed and adopted or rejected by various courts.

C. Uniform Laws (Annotated)

Everyone has heard of the Uniform Commercial Code and the Model Penal Code. These are not themselves law, but they were drafted for state legislatures to adopt their provisions as state statutes.

Researchers should know that when the same language is adopted in another state's statutes, a court decision interpreting that identical language may be especially persuasive to an Illinois court. The *Uniform Laws Annotated* allows researchers to see which jurisdictions have adopted the proposed uniform laws, whether the state legislatures amended any of the proposed statutory language, and how courts of the various jurisdictions have interpreted particular provisions.

D. A.L.R. Annotations

The *American Law Reports* contain leading cases and articles that describe how the same legal issue is treated in other jurisdictions. The articles are usually not critical but objectively descriptive of the national legal landscape on a particular legal topic. You can use the A.L.R. annotations to see, for example, whether a particular Illinois case represents the majority or minority rule in other jurisdictions in the United States. The series is updated regularly and it has a comprehensive set of index volumes. Footnotes in *A.L.R.* annotations can also be a rich source of cases on point.[35]

---

35. See Jean McKnight, *Researching Illinois Court Opinions*, 85 Ill. B.J. 445, 446 (1997).

You may locate an annotation in the *American Law Reports* by using the index, but you are often more likely to encounter a reference to an *A.L.R.* annotation when you are Shepardizing the cases that you cite. If you are lucky enough to locate an *A.L.R.* annotation this way, you will find useful information about the cases you are citing.

VII. Chapter Summary

Secondary sources may provide you with an overview of the law, explanations of various rules of law, and citations to primary authorities. Researchers in an unfamiliar area of the law are often best advised to consult secondary sources first. Although they may not control the result of your legal issue, they will show you what that result should be and how to best reach it.

Additional Resources

Busharis, Barbara J. and Suzanne E. Rowe.^ *Florida Legal Research: Sources, Process, and Analysis* 125–54 (2d ed., Carolina Academic Press 2002).

Duggan, James E. *Illinois Bar Association Journals and Newsletters,* 88 Ill. B.J. 175 (2000).

Duggan, James E. *Using Illinois Legal Encyclopedias,* 87 Ill. B.J. 167 (1999).

Duggan, James E. *Legal Newspapers and Law Reviews: Focus on Illinois Law,* 88 Ill. B.J. 49 (2000).

Duggan, James E. *Evidence Practice Guides,* 88 Ill. B.J. 543 (2000).

Kunz, Christina L., Deborah A. Schmedemann, Matthew P. Downs, and Ann L. Bateson. *The Process of Legal Research* 49–107 (5th ed., Aspen L. & Bus. 2000).

Houdek, Frank & Jean McKnight, *Survey of Illinois Law: An Annotated Bibliography of Legal Research Tools*, 16 S. Ill. U. L.J. 767, 776–801 (1992).

McKnight, Jean. *Researching Illinois Law in Periodicals*, 86 Ill. B.J. 279, 279 (1998).

Mersky, Roy M. and Donald J. Dunn, *Fundamentals of Legal Research* 350–426 (8th ed., Foundation Press 2002).

Sloan, Amy E. *Basic Legal Research: Tools and Strategies* 25–72 (2d ed., Aspen Publishers 2003).

Svengalis, Kendall F. *Legal Information and Buyer's Guide and Reference Manual* (Rhode Island LawPress 2002).

Wendt, Laurel. *Illinois Legal Research Manual* 205–13 (Butterworth Legal Publishers 1988).

Chapter 8

Rules of Court and Rules of Ethics

I. Introduction

Court rules govern the procedures that lawyers must follow in civil and criminal litigation, and when appealing to higher courts.[1] The general purpose of the Illinois Court Rules is "to facilitate the orderly disposition of the business of [the] courts and to expedite the prompt administration of justice."[2] Lawyers know that successful litigation depends upon knowing the applicable rules. They also know that "[t]here may be a high cost for non-compliance with procedural rules," including possible dismissal of a case.[3] In Illinois state courts, the court rules include the rules of civil procedure, appellate procedure, and professional conduct for attorneys and judges. In addition to these state rules, there may be local court rules that apply to your case.[4]

---

1. *See e.g.* Barbara J. Busharis & Suzanne E. Rowe, *Florida Legal Research: Sources, Process, and Analysis* 155 (2d ed., Carolina Academic Press 2002).
2. *Sawyier v. Young*, 556 N.E.2d 759, 762 (Ill. App. 1st Dist. 1990).
3. Carole C. Berry, *Effective Appellate Advocacy: Brief Writing and Oral Argument* 68 (3d ed., West Group 2003).
4. *See e.g.* DuPage County Bar Assn., *Rules of the Circuit Court of the Eighteenth Judicial Circuit* (1999).

The Illinois Supreme Court has the power to make rules of pleading, practice, and procedure for all Illinois courts to supplement rules found in the Illinois Code of Civil Procedure.[5] And subject to rules of the Illinois Supreme Court, the Circuit and Appellate Courts may make their own rules to regulate their dockets, court calendars, and judicial business.[6]

II. Researching Illinois Court Rules

A. Finding the Text of Court Rules

Illinois court rules can be found in volumes accompanying the Illinois Compiled Statutes. The *Illinois Compiled Statutes Annotated* published by LexisNexis and the *Smith-Hurd Illinois Compiled Statutes Annotated* published by West Group are both reliable and easy to use.

Some Illinois court rules are also published in separate volumes that lawyers will bring to court.[7] Illinois Supreme Court rules are also published in the *Illinois Reports,* which is a useful source for doing historical research on particular rules. Volumes containing amended Illinois Supreme Court Rules are easily identifiable by looking at the spines of the bound volumes of the *Illinois Reports.*

Some rules, such as the rules of professional responsibility, can also be found published in free booklets. The rules governing the legal profession and judiciary in Illinois are available in a free publi-

---

5. *See* Heija B. Ryoo, *Illinois Judicial Circuit Court Rules 1999: A Working Bibliography*, 87 Ill. B.J. 669 (1999).
6. *See id.*
7. These publications include the Law Bulletin Publishing Company's *Illinois Courts Rule Book*, the West Group's *Illinois Court Rules and Procedure*, and the West Group's *Illinois Criminal Law and Procedure.*

cation from the Attorney Registration and Disciplinary Commission of the Illinois Supreme Court.[8] This is not the only source for finding these rules, but it is convenient and free. The publication includes the Illinois Rules of Judicial Conduct, the Illinois Supreme Court Rules on the Admission and Discipline of Attorneys, the Illinois Rules of Professional Conduct, the Rules of the Attorney Registration and Disciplinary Commission, and the Rules of the Board of Admissions and Committee on Character and Fitness.

Visitors to the official website of the Illinois Supreme Court can subscribe to a free service that will send e-mail notices of changes to the Illinois Supreme Court Rules.[9] This service is an important one, as changes to the rules can affect pending cases.

B. Finding Judicial Interpretations of the Court Rules

On the federal level, cases interpreting the federal rules are frequently found in a special reporter, the *Federal Rules Decisions*. The "F.R.D." also includes law review articles and proceedings from judicial conferences where the federal rules are discussed.

There is not a similar reporter for rules of the Illinois courts. Nevertheless, cases interpreting Illinois rules are easy to find in the annotated statutes. The *Illinois Compiled Statutes Annotated* pub-

---

8. The Attorney Registration and Disciplinary Commission can be contacted at 130 E. Randolph Drive, Suite 1500, Chicago, IL 60601 or at One North Old Capitol Plaza, Suite 333, Springfield, IL 62701. Further information is also available at www.iardc.org.

9. http://www.state.il.us/court/SupremeCourt/Rules/SubRules.htm. Visitors to the website can also elect to receive e-mail notices of cases where the court grants leave to appeal. This information is important to researchers, who must know whether the appellate court decision they are citing is subject to further review. E-mail notices are also available for anticipated filings of opinions, so that you can be among the first to know when the court has issued a new ruling in a particular case.

lished by LexisNexis and the *Smith-Hurd Illinois Compiled Statutes Annotated* published by West Group both contain case annotations where Illinois courts have interpreted and applied the various rules.

Cases interpreting particular Illinois court rules can also be found by Shepardizing those court rules in the *Shepard's Illinois Citations*. When interpreting an Illinois Supreme Court Rule, the courts will consider "the reasons and necessity for [enacting the rule], the evil to be remedied, and the purpose of the rule."[10] It is possible to Shepardize not only the rules promulgated by the Illinois Supreme Court, but also local court rules and general orders, including rules and general orders of the Circuit Court of Cook County (and its Probate Division, Criminal Division, County Division, and Municipal Department).

C. Finding Commentary on the Court Rules

The most important commentary on court rules is the Committee Comments from those who drafted the court rules. The *Illinois Compiled Statutes Annotated* and the *Smith-Hurd Illinois Compiled Statutes Annotated* both include the text of official committee comments. They also include citations to law review commentary on particular rules.

Some rules may be the subject of extensive commentary. Rule 23, for example, is a controversial rule that prohibits lawyers from citing certain appellate court decisions, even when they are directly on point and even if there is no other published authority available to cite.[11] Bar association journals and newsletters should not be ignored as sources of commentary on particular Illinois court rules.

---

10. *Gibson v. Belvidere Natl. Bank & Trust*, 759 N.E.2d 991, 996 (Ill. App. 2d Dist. 2001), *appeal denied*, 770 N.E.2d 218 (Ill. 2002).

11. *See e.g.* Michael T. Reagan, *Supreme Court Rule 23: The Terrain of the Debate and a Proposed Revision*, 90 Ill. B.J. 180 (2002).

III. Rules of Ethics

A. Ethical Rules for Judges

1. Substantive Rules

The behavior of judges is governed by the *Illinois Code of Judicial Conduct*. Rules in that code can be shepardized in the *Shepards' Illinois Citations* to find cases that have interpreted and applied the rules.

2. Illinois Courts Commission

The Illinois Courts Commission is the body that disciplines judges. It reviews complaints filed by the Judicial Inquiry Board, a body created by the 1970 Illinois Constitution.[12]

Decisions of the Commission are published in the *Illinois Courts Commission Reports*. The Commission may remove a judge from office or otherwise reprimand a judge for willful misconduct in office, persistent failure to perform judicial duties, or for other conduct that is prejudicial to the administration of justice.[13]

B. Ethical Rules for Attorneys

1. Substantive Rules

Attorneys are governed by the Illinois Rules of Professional Conduct and the Illinois Supreme Court Rules on the Admission and Discipline of Attorneys. Copies can be found in many sources, including with the annotated statutes. These rules of ethics can be shepardized in the *Shepards' Illinois Citations* to find cases that have interpreted and applied the rules.

---

12. Ill. Const. art. VI, § 15(e) (as amended Nov. 3, 1998).
13. *Id.*

Although the rules apply to attorneys, they also apply to everyone who works for an attorney as well. Attorneys who educate their support staffs about the ethical rules (such as the duty to preserve client confidences) "are less likely to suffer ethical lapses in their offices."[14]

Illinois attorneys must comply with the Rules of Professional Conduct, and they are also under an affirmative obligation to report misconduct of other attorneys.[15]

2. Illinois Attorney Registration and Disciplinary Commission

The body that disciplines lawyers is the Attorney Registration and Disciplinary Commission of the Illinois Supreme Court (the "ARDC"). Summary reports of disciplinary proceedings are published in publications such as the *Chicago Daily Law Bulletin*, where all your friends from law school will read about the ethical violations you may have committed.

The Illinois Supreme Court established the Attorney Registration and Disciplinary Commission to administer the registration of all lawyers in Illinois and to investigate complaints of attorney misconduct.[16] The ARDC thus is often called upon to interpret the rules and apply them to the factual situations that come before the Commission. If you have a question about the rules of ethics that cannot be answered just by looking at the Rules of Professional Conduct, the Commission maintains an Ethics Inquiry Program. This is a

---

14. Anne E. Thar, *Legal Malpractice, Ethics, and Your Support Staff*, 88 Ill. B.J. 603 (2000).
15. *See In re Himmel*, 533 N.E.2d 790, 796 (Ill. 1988) (attorney suspended for one year for failing to report the misconduct of another attorney).
16. *See* Mary F. Andreoni, *Practicing Ethically*, at 1–3, in *Starting Points: The Fundamentals of Practice in Illinois* (Ill. Inst. for CLE 2001).

telephone line enquiry where lawyers can ask senior lawyers at the ARDC hypothetical questions and receive informal guidance.[17]

C. Bar Association Ethics Opinions

Several bar associations publish ethics advisory opinions that are not binding, but are highly persuasive and tremendously helpful to attorneys who want to avoid specific ethical dilemmas.[18] The Illinois State Bar Association is a voluntary bar association with no particular authority over enforcing or interpreting the ethical rules. The ISBA does, however, publish a series of ethics opinions that provide authoritative guidance on interpretation of the ethical rules applicable to lawyers and judges in Illinois.[19] Opinions are also published in the *Illinois Bar Journal.*

The Chicago Bar Association's Professional Responsibility Committee has also issued its own legal ethics opinions "as a public service to aid lawyers in interpreting the Illinois Rules of Professional Conduct."[20]

The American Bar Association also maintains a staff of lawyers experienced in legal ethics research, and their services are typically available at no charge to any lawyer or judge, regardless of whether he or she is a member of the ABA.[21]

---

17. *See id.* at 1–13. Lawyers can call the ethics hotline in Chicago at (800) 826-8625 or in Springfield at (800) 252-8048. You can also request copies of the rules and other publications, such as Mary Robinson, *Avoiding ARDC Anxiety: A Disciplinary Primer*, 84 Ill. B.J. 452 (1996).
18. Jean McKnight, *Researching Legal Ethics in Illinois*, 86 Ill. B.J. 509, 509 (1998).
19. Copies of ISBA Ethics Opinions are available in print, on the web at www.isba.org, or on Westlaw in the "ILETH-EO" database. Opinions are also available by calling the Illinois State Bar Association at (800) 252-8908.
20. *CBA Committee Offers New Ethics Opinions*, 11 CBA Rec. 44, 44 (June/July 1997).
21. For more information call (800) 285-2221 (ext. 8) or email ethicsearch@staff.abanet.org. You can also visit the website at www.abanet.org/cpr/ethicsearch.

IV. Updating Ethical Rules

The ABA's formal and informal ethics opinions, the Code of Professional Responsibility, the Model Rules of Professional Conduct, and the Code of Judicial Conduct can be Shepardized in *Shepard's Professional and Judicial Conduct Citations*.[22] They can also be checked in *Shepard's Illinois Citations*.[23]

V. Researching Local Federal Rules

The U.S. Court of Appeals for the Seventh Circuit covers the geographic areas of Illinois, Indiana, and Wisconsin. Local rules for the Seventh Circuit can be found in a number of sources, but it is generally agreed that a reliable source of current rules is to be found on the court's website at http://www.ca7.uscourts.gov/. The website features include the federal rules and local rules for the Seventh Circuit, a useful *Practitioner's Handbook for Appeals*, sample briefs, and other important information about the court.

Local rules for the federal district courts, and the federal bankruptcy courts in Illinois, can be found on the websites for each court.[24] The websites include information on the court, the judges, local rules, forms, recent decisions and orders. Of special interest to law students is information on judges who are hiring law clerks.

---

22. Jean McKnight, *Researching Legal Ethics in Illinois*, 86 Ill. B.J. 509, 510 (1998).
23. *Id.*
24. *See* Appendix A.

Additional Resources

Andreoni, Mary F. *Practicing Ethically,* in *Starting Points: The Fundamentals of Practice in Illinois* ch. 1 (Ill. Inst. for CLE 2001).

Busharis, Barbara J. & Suzanne E. Rowe. *Florida Legal Research: Sources, Process, and Analysis* 155–63 (2d ed., Carolina Academic Press 2002).

Collins, Maureen B. *E-mail and Attorney Client Communications,* 88 Ill. B.J. 541 (2000).

Dilibert, Karen J. *Ten Tips for Responding to an ARDC Inquiry,* 89 Ill. B.J. 213 (2001).

Garner, Bryan A. *Guidelines for Drafting and Editing Court Rules,* 169 F.R.D. 176 (1997).

Grant, Todd W. *Resources for Research in Legal Ethics* (William S. Hein & Co. 1992) (volume 13 of the Legal Research Guide Series).

Hopkins, Kevin. *Law Firms, Technology, and The Double-Billing Dilemma,* 12 Georgetown J. Legal Ethics 95 (1998).

The John Marshall Law School Ethics Advisory Service, *Opinions and Index* (1993).

Lee, David L. & Sarah R. Masarachia, *"Kiss My Grits" and Other Eloquent Retorts: Incivility in Legal Writing,* 13 CBA Rec. 28 (Apr. 1999).

McKnight, Jean. *Researching Legal Ethics in Illinois,* 86 Ill. B.J. 509 (1998).

Mulroy, Thomas R., Jr., ed., *Annotated Guide to the Illinois Rules of Professional Conduct* (Ill. Inst. for CLE 1991).

Reavy, Patrick G. *Legal Malpractice: A Research Guide for Lawyers and Law Students* (William S. Hein & Co. 1995) (volume 24 of the Legal Research Guide Series).

Ryoo, Heija B. *Illinois Judicial Circuit Court Rules 1999: A Working Bibliography,* 87 Ill. B.J. 669 (1999).

Sloan, Amy E. *Basic Legal Research: Tools and Strategies* 168–69 (2d ed., Aspen Publishers 2003).

Thar, Anne E. *Legal Malpractice, Ethics, and Your Support Staff,* 88 Ill. B.J. 603 (2000).

Vande Werken, Walter B. & Debra Lynn Adamo. *Illinois Courts Rule Book* (4th ed., Law Bulletin Publishing Co. 2002).

Wendt, Laurel. *Illinois Legal Research Manual* 219–28 (Butterworth Legal Publishers 1988).

Chapter 9

Form Books, Forms, and Jury Instructions

I. Introduction

Form books serve a special function for research and drafting. There are many types of form books, including forms for civil litigation, attorney-client retainer agreements, contracts, deeds, leases, powers of attorney, trusts, wills, and many other matters. No one likes to reinvent the wheel, and this includes lawyers who must draft documents that may be similar to documents that others have drafted previously.[1]

It is quite common to use forms to draft all sorts of documents. I once taught a special drafting course for lawyers who worked at one of the largest law firms in the world. Part of that course required the lawyers to submit samples of "original drafting" that they had done. Most of the writing samples submitted, however, were not "original drafting," but were filled in forms modeled from earlier documents.

The use of form books (or "precedents" as they might say in the United Kingdom) is not necessarily a bad thing if the forms are

---

1. *See* Barbara J. Busharis & Suzanne E. Rowe, *Florida Legal Research: Sources, Process, and Analysis* 165 (2d ed., Carolina Academic Press 2002).

well written and serve the needs of the client. However, not all form books are created equal. You must be sure that you understand every word of the form you are using, and that you understand why that word is there. You must take care to see that the form protects your client while being fair to the other side. You must also confirm that the forms you are using comply with Illinois law.[2] A form taken from another jurisdiction may not be valid under Illinois law.

To some extent, well-written form books will help you with the research that you need to understand the forms. A book such as *Illinois Forms: Legal and Business*, for example, includes not only the forms, but also commentary about the legal issues related to using the forms. This commentary includes general considerations about drafting and alerts you to various other concerns, such as potential tax issues. The form books also offer citations to primary and secondary sources that you may need to consult for your research. You should not only consult the primary sources referenced – you should Shepardize them as well.

Barbara Busharis and Suzanne Rowe offer some useful advice on using form books:

> Form books are most useful when drafting any type of document for the first time. While you are unlikely to find a form that is exactly like the document you are trying to draft, form books offer a starting point for unfamiliar territory. In addition to the actual forms, form books often include helpful commentary about the forms, cross references to secondary sources, and explanatory notes. Also very helpful are checklists of information you need to complete the forms and related legal matters you should consider.[3]

---

2. The language of some Illinois forms may be required by statute.
3. Busharis & Rowe, *supra* note 1, at 165–66.

II. How to Use Form Books

A. Research First

Before you use any form, you must do the legal research necessary to be sure that you are using the correct form, and that you are using it correctly. If you do not understand a provision in a form that you are using as a model, you must do the research necessary to find out what the provision means. Doing the necessary research will help you identify any provisions in the form that may be inappropriate for your client, as well as any provisions that may be affected by recent developments in the law. For example, a change in the tax law could adversely affect your client, or at least deprive your client of a benefit.

Luckily, many form books contain specific references to relevant primary authorities, commentary on those authorities, and references to secondary sources. Again, you should not only read the primary sources referenced, you must update them as well to be sure there are no developments that may affect your clients.

B. Take Care When Combining Provisions

It is common to combine provisions from different forms, and from different form books. The reason for this is that few forms cover every aspect of a client's problem. Additionally, lawyers know that every case is unique in some way. There is some additional fact, or some additional goal, that the client wants to achieve. Consequently, a lawyer must take care when combining provisions from different forms.

Problems may arise, for example, when a lawyer combines provisions from different commercial contracts. Some contracts are drafted to favor sellers. Some contracts are drafted to favor buyers. However, a lawyer who does not understand which provisions favor which side may inadvertently combine conflicting provisions from competing forms. The conflicting provisions may escape everyone's notice until a contract dispute arises. By that time, of course, it is too late to fix the drafting problem, and the parties to the contract are left to litigate their differences.

Not all of the forms you will find will be well drafted. Look for ways of improving the forms you find. The new document that you draft may well become the model for a future form book.

III. Finding Illinois Form Books

Many of the national form books have forms that may be used in Illinois.[4] These include form books for litigation, forming corporations, drafting leases, or drafting contracts. The John Marshall Law School Law Library publishes a useful *Research Guide for Form Books* that includes many of these national titles, as well as specific subject matter titles. Also included in that publication is a list of form books for general Illinois practice, and for specific subjects areas under Illinois law. Other law libraries may have similar lists of form books.

Form books can be found by using the library catalog. A search term such as "forms" should produce a large number of results. You may search for forms in particular areas by combining your search with particular words, such as "commercial law" and "forms." For state-specific forms, you can include "Illinois" as an additional search term.

Another tool to consult is *West's Illinois Law Finder*, a reference guide that will direct you to specific sections of from books published by the West Group. You can look under "Forms" in the *West's Illinois Law Finder*, or under specific subject-matter listings that will include form books among the resources cited. The only drawback

---

4. A selection of general form books includes *American Jurisprudence Legal Forms* and West's *Legal Forms*.

Form Books, Forms, and Jury Instructions • 163

is that it will refer you only to form books published by the West Group, leaving out many other publications. But the *West's Illinois Law Finder* is nonetheless a valuable tool, and it will direct you to state-specific form books and general form books with materials that can be used in Illinois.

A publication such as *West's Illinois Forms* will include volumes on civil practice and domestic relations. In addition to the forms themselves, the publication summarizes the applicable law and includes bibliographic references to secondary sources and an index. Other Illinois-specific form books that you may find include:

- Bernard B. Rinella & Richard A. Rinella, *Illinois Domestic Relations Forms* (Lexis Law Publishing 1992).
- Chris E. Freese & Timothy E. Duggan, *Illinois Client Interview Forms* (Ill. State Bar Assn. 2001).
- Paul D. Rudnick, Gregory W. Hummel, & Paul E. Fisher, *Illinois Real Estate Forms* (Lexis Law Publishing 1989).
- Richard G. Goldenhersh & Timothy W. Kelly, eds., *Illinois Causes of Action – Elements, Forms & Winning Tips: Tort Actions* (Ill. Inst. for CLE 2002).
- Richard G. Goldenhersh & Timothy W. Kelly, eds., *Illinois Causes of Action – Elements, Forms & Winning Tips: Estate, Business, and Non-Personal Injury Actions* (Ill. Inst. for CLE 2002).
- Ronald P. Given, *Illinois Commercial Financing Forms* (Butterworth Legal Publishers 1992).
- Thomas A. Abendroth, *Illinois Estate Planning, Will Drafting, and Estate Administration Forms* (3d ed., Lexis Law Publishing 1999).
- William Alexander Price, *Illinois Law Office Practice Forms* (Michie Butterworth 1995).

In addition to these Illinois-specific form books, other Illinois forms may be found as part of general CLE materials. A chapter on Domestic Relations in an IICLE Handbook, for example, includes samples of a basic intake form, an attorney engagement agreement (including a statement of the client's rights and responsibilities), a motion for temporary support and maintenance, and various discovery requests.[5]

IV. Legal Forms from Cyberspace

The Internet offers many legal forms, often to individuals who hope to avoid using lawyers.[6] Many forms are written as though they can be used in multiple jurisdictions, ignoring specific requirements or developments in the laws of a particular state. Many of the available forms can be used of course, but they must be used with caution and only after doing the basic research necessary to understand which forms to use and how to use them.

Some Internet sites for legal forms include:
- http://www.lexisone.com/
- http://www.findlaw.com/16forms/index.html/
- http://www.allaboutforms.com/
- http://www.uslegalforms.com/illinois/
- http://www.washlaw.edu/legalforms/legalforms.html/
- http://www.findlegalforms.com/

V. Federal Court Forms

Some forms that you will need as a lawyer are available from the courts and administrative agencies where you will practice. Lawyers who practice immigration, customs, or bankruptcy law, for example, must be very familiar with a wide variety of forms. Sample

---

5. Steven N. Peskind, *Domestic Relations*, at 2-41 to 2-90 in *Starting Points: The Fundamentals of Practice in Illinois* (Ill. Inst. for CLE 2001).

6. Individuals who use these forms incorrectly often later generate a good deal of business for lawyers.

forms are available in form books and are usually also available directly from the court or agency.

Although this book is focused on state materials, it should be noted that there are federal forms available on the website for the U.S. Court of Appeals for the Seventh Circuit.[7] The website does not include the wide range of forms found in form books. It does, however, include sample briefs and various court forms. Many new attorneys have secretly consulted the sample forms for *pro se* petitioners, just to be sure that they have not forgotten anything when filling out their own forms.

You can find local forms (and local rules) on the websites for the federal district courts of Illinois. The federal bankruptcy courts also have local rules and local forms on their websites.[8]

VI. Illinois Jury Instructions

Jury instructions are, simply, the instructions given to the jury at the end of a trial. There are special form books with pattern jury instructions, but most practitioners have never opened one of them. That may be a mistake. If you know what instructions a jury will receive at the end of the trial, then you know what you must prove at trial in order to win. Having this specific information allows you to focus your research on precisely what it is that you need to win.

Why do most attorneys neglect the pattern jury instructions as a research tool? Most cases never go to trial. And of those cases that do go to trial, many settle. The need to prepare jury instructions may seem to be only a remote possibility; in this light, consulting the pattern jury instructions may seem to be an endeavor unworthy of the attorney's time. But if you did consult the jury instructions, your confidence in preparing for trial would increase. You would

---

7. The website can be found at http://www.ca7.uscourts.gov/.
8. *See* Appendix A.

also be more confident in settlement negotiations, because you would know that you can satisfy each of the tests that the jury will be asked to apply at the end of the trial. The pattern jury instructions are an overlooked research resource that you should consult well before the trial starts, and probably before you ever file the complaint.

There are two main sets of jury instructions for Illinois, one for civil trials,[9] and one for criminal trials.[10] The pattern jury instructions include the instructions, notes on their use, and commentary with citations to legal authority. If the pattern jury instructions do not have what you need, you can consult the non-pattern instructions that may fill in the gaps.[11]

Illinois jury instructions can be Shepardized in the *Shepard's Illinois Citations*. Taking this simple and necessary step will alert you to likely arguments and potential problems that may arise in connection with particular jury instructions.

Additional Resources

Balough, Richard C. *Drafting Contract Provisions for E-Commerce Sites*, 88 Ill. B.J. 40 (2000).

Busharis, Barbara J. and Suzanne E. Rowe. *Florida Legal Research: Sources, Process, and Analysis* 165–172 (2d ed., Carolina Academic Press 2002).

Houdek, Frank & Jean McKnight. *Survey of Illinois Law: An Annotated Bibliography of Legal Research Tools*, 16 S. Ill. U. L.J. 767, 769–70 (1992).

---

9. Illinois Supreme Court Commission on Pattern Jury Instructions in Civil Cases, *Illinois Pattern Jury Instructions: Civil* (West Group 2000).

10. Illinois Supreme Court Commission on Pattern Jury Instructions in Criminal Cases, *Illinois Pattern Jury Instructions: Criminal* (4th ed., West Group 2000).

11. *See e.g.* Carl L. Rowley & Jon M. Moyers, *Illinois Non-Pattern Jury Instructions* (3d ed., West Group 2001).

The John Marshall Law School Law Library. *Research Guide for Form Books* (2001).

Johnson, Phill. *How to Find Jury Instructions*, 91 Ill. B.J. 361 (2003).

Olmi, Adria P. *Real-Estate Resources on the Internet for Illinois Lawyers*, 89 Ill. B.J. 495 (2001).

Sorkin, David E. *Not the Same Old Complaint*, 83 Ill. B.J. 201 (1995).

Svengalis, Kendall F. *Legal Information and Buyer's Guide and Reference Manual* (Rhode Island LawPress 2002).

Wendt, Laurel. *Illinois Legal Research Manual* 229–50 (Butterworth Legal Publishers 1988).

Chapter 10

Looseleaf Services

I. Introduction

A law librarian recently expressed surprise to me that a third-year law student who was about to graduate claimed to have never heard of a "looseleaf service." The soon-to-be-lawyer knew about Westlaw and LexisNexis, of course, but he was entirely oblivious to these specialized reporters. For this librarian, and for many practitioners, looseleaf services provide an indispensable resource for specific practice areas.

Looseleaf services are a special combination of primary and secondary authority related to specific subject areas of the law.[1] For example, the *Illinois Public Employee Reporter* collects judicial and administrative decisions, such as decisions of the Illinois Educational Labor Relations Board, the Illinois ELRB Executive Director, and the Illinois Labor Relations Board.[2]

Looseleaf services are published by a variety of publishers, on a variety of subjects, and in a variety of formats. They collectively became known as "looseleaf services" because many of the publications

---

1. *See generally* Barbara J. Busharis & Suzanne E. Rowe, *Florida Legal Research: Sources, Process, and Analysis* 173-79 (2d ed., Carolina Academic Press 2002); Amy E. Sloan, *Basic Legal Research: Tools and Strategies* 267-92 (2d ed., Aspen Publishers 2003).
2. Information about the *Illinois Public Employee Reporter* is available from LRP Publications, 747 Dresher Road, P.O. Box 980, Horsham, PA 19044-0980; tel. (215) 784-0860.

were first published in looseleaf binders.[3] They have also been called "mini-libraries" on particular subject matter areas.[4] That may be a better term to describe these services, particularly as a service published on CD-ROM is hard to think of as a "looseleaf service." Others have called these services "Reporter Services."[5]

These publications include, in one or more volumes, a collection of primary authority related to a specific subject area. They may include judicial decisions from many jurisdictions, but only for one particular subject matter.[6] These publications may also include statutes, legislative history, regulations, administrative law decisions, constitutional provisions, and excerpts from relevant international sources such as treaties. They may include information about proposed legislation or comments submitted on proposed regulations. All of the information may include both state and federal sources.

Many of the looseleaf services include their own commentary on specific legal developments or on the need for legal reforms in a particular area. They may include citations to (or summaries of) relevant law review articles and other secondary sources. These publications may also include sample forms and other materials useful to practitioners and researchers.

Because these publications often include materials from several jurisdictions, researchers may not think of looseleaf services as being particularly valuable for a research problem involving only Illinois law. But for a researcher in Illinois with a specific legal problem, it is indeed helpful to know all of the major legal developments from other jurisdictions. It is possible to recreate much of this material by

---

3. *See* Sloan, *supra* note 1, at 268.
4. *See* Christina L. Kunz, Deborah A. Schmedemann, Matthew P. Downs, & Ann L. Bateson, *The Process of Legal Research* 306 (5th ed., Aspen L. & Bus. 2000).
5. *See e.g. Reporter Services and Their Uses* (2d ed., Bureau of Natl. Affairs, Inc. 1989). The book describes these services as "an important legal research tool that is often neglected during the hectic law school years." *Id.* at vii.
6. *See* Sloan, *supra* note 1, at 267.

searching various databases, but it is so much easier to use a tool that someone else has already created.

Christina Kunz and her colleagues offer four good reasons to use "mini-libraries" for legal research. First, they note that these services promote efficiency because they allow you to cover "a range of authorities within a single source."[7] You can consult cases, statutes, regulations, legislative histories, administrative materials, and summaries of secondary sources all within the same book. Second, they note that the "sharp editorial focus" on one specific area of the law allows to you do "focused research."[8] You will not be distracted or overwhelmed by research materials not relating to your immediate problem. Third, they note that "a mini-library contains material not easily available elsewhere; this promotes comprehensive research."[9] You may find, for example, an explanatory letter from the head of an administrative agency. There may be no other place where that letter is published, and that letter may have the key to your legal research problem. Fourth, they note that materials in a looseleaf service are kept current, and that "the current information may be integrated into the older material."[10] This will save you time that you would otherwise spend updating older materials that you find.

II. Finding Looseleaf Services

There are several ways of finding looseleaf services.

First, a legal citation manual such as *The Bluebook* contains a list of looseleaf services in Table 16. You can browse through this list to find looseleaf services that will be helpful to you.

Second, you can search the publication called *Legal Looseleafs in*

---

7. *See* Kunz, *supra* note 4, at 307.
8. *Id.*
9. *Id.*
10. *Id.*

Print,[11] and the related *Directory of Law-Related CD-ROMs.*[12] Thomas Keefe, librarian at The John Marshall Law School Law Library, recommends the *Legal Information Buyer's Guide & Reference Manual*[13] for any law firms that are interested in cost-effective acquisition of legal reference materials. The book compares prices of different services and shows many alterative methods of finding necessary information, including looseleaf services.

Third, you can ask the reference librarian to help you locate a looseleaf service related to your research problem. You may also contact the publishers of looseleaf services, who will be more than happy to send you information about how to purchase their products.

III. Using Looseleaf Services in Print

When you find a looseleaf service, look for material (usually at the front of the first volume) that describes "how to use" the particular service. Then read that. You will find detailed explanations of the special features and finding tools particular to that looseleaf service, as well as a description of the primary and secondary sources in it. It will also explain any special research suggestions for effective use of the particular publication.

IV. Citing Looseleaf Services

A researcher who finds a primary source (such as a court opinion or administrative law decision) in a looseleaf service would not nor-

---

11. Arlene L. Eis, *Legal Looseleafs in Print 2002* (Infosources Publishing 2002).

12. Arlene L. Eis, *Directory of Law-Related CD-ROMs 2002* (Infosources Publishing 2002).

13. Kendall F. Svengalis, *Legal Information Buyer's Guide & Reference Manual* (Rhode Island LawPress 2002).

mally cite to the looseleaf reporter. Instead, the researcher would cite to an official or regional reporter.

There are three exceptions to this general rule.

First, a decision in a looseleaf service may not yet be published in an official reporter. The looseleaf reporter may be the best source of many decisions, such as administrative law decisions. In these instances, the researcher should cite to the looseleaf service.

Second, the material in a looseleaf reporter may not be reported elsewhere. You may be citing an administrative law decision or memorandum that is not published elsewhere. Additionally, commentary written for the specific looseleaf reporter will not be available in other sources. The researcher must cite to the looseleaf service when it is the only place to find the material.

Third, a researcher should cite to a looseleaf reporter when it is known that the specific reader of the memorandum or brief has easy access to that specific reporter. In these instances, citing to the looseleaf service provides readers with the immediate ability to use the same resource.

V. Using Computerized Databases as Looseleaf Services

Looseleaf services are increasingly available online to subscribers who pay for access. Because of the ease of updating materials, Internet-based services also appear to be replacing many CD-ROM publications.[14]

Researchers should not make the mistake of thinking that a general Internet search (using a search engine such as Google, for example) is the same as using an Internet-based looseleaf service. With general Internet searches, you will always have problems determin-

---

14. *See* Sloan, *supra* note 1, at 275.

ing the completeness and accuracy of material that you find. You can certainly use the Internet as a starting point for much research,[15] but whatever you find must be independently confirmed from reliable sources.

Computerized research services such as Westlaw and Lexis Nexis may also be used as looseleaf services, although they will not include the special editorial enhancements particular to many looseleaf services. Nevertheless, both of these services will allow you to search by practice or topic areas and to combine searches of cases, statutes, regulations, and secondary sources. [16]

Using an electronic-based service will be convenient, but remember that the main value of print-based looseleaf services is that they collect almost everything you will need in a particular practice area. If you are the person designated to file the updates when they come in, you will soon find that you are the person with the most current knowledge on changes in the law.

Additional Resources

Busharis, Barbara J. & Suzanne E. Rowe, *Florida Legal Research: Sources, Process, and Analysis* 173-79 (2d ed., Carolina Academic Press 2002).

Eis, Arlene L. *Directory of Law-Related CD-ROMs 2002* (Infosources Publishing 2002).

Eis, Arlene L. *Legal Looseleafs in Print 2002* (Infosources Publishing 2002).

---

15. *See id.* at 276.
16. *See id.* at 278. Westlaw will allow you to search "Topical Materials by Area of Practice." Lexis will allow you to search "Area of Law by Topic." *See id.*

Kunz, Christina L., Deborah A. Schmedemann, Matthew P. Downs, & Ann L. Bateson, *The Process of Legal Research* 306-22 (5th ed., Aspen L. & Bus. 2000).

LeBlanc, Mary Ellen, & John M. Rossi, eds., *The Internet Guide for Illinois Lawyers* (Ill. Inst. for CLE 1997).

Sloan, Amy E. *Basic Legal Research: Tools and Strategies* 267-92 (2d ed., Aspen Publishers 2003).

Chapter 11

Legal Citation

I. Six Citation Functions

Legal citations serve at least six important functions in legal writing.

A. Establish Authority

As much as we would like to think otherwise, just because you write something will not necessary make it so. Citations show that a binding court decision, statute, regulation, or other source of legal authority supports a proposition advanced on behalf of a client. Indeed, "[t]he notion that citation to authority is necessary seems almost inescapable in a legal system based on precedent."[1] Citations allow the reader to determine the level of support for a particular proposition of law. A reader can see, for example, whether a particular authority cited is binding or merely persuasive.

B. Minimize Distraction

I wear a suit when I appear in court. I have never found a rule that says that I must wear a suit, it is simply something that I do be-

---

1. *See* Michael Bacchus, Student Author, *Strung Out: Legal Citation, the Bluebook, and the Anxiety of Authority*, 151 U. Pa. L. Rev. 245, 254 (2002).

cause it is expected of me. A judge who does not see me in a suit will be distracted by my appearance and miss the point of my argument. Because a certain appearance is expected, I comply with that expectation.

Similarly, if there is something wrong with the appearance of my citations in a brief, the reader may be distracted from the substance of my argument. An improper citation form may damage my credibility as a lawyer. Although the process of using correct legal citations may seem to be tedious one, the citations in my written work must conform to the expected rules of citation. A proper legal citation will "minimize distraction."[2]

C. Ensure Accuracy

Proper citations allow readers to consult the original sources and ensure that the authority is being cited correctly. Judges, law clerks, and attorneys for the other side will check the accuracy of the authorities you cite. The reader may also use the citation to locate additional information that may be necessary for proper analysis of a legal issue.

D. Avoid Plagiarism

Proper citation of authority avoids potential problems of plagiarism when a writer acknowledges the original source of an idea or the particular expression of an idea. This reflects the basic idea that "citation is a structure of indebtedness" and that the purpose of citation is "simple attribution of ideas and expressions of ideas to authority outside of a specific text."[3]

Although proper citation may not be of concern to a lawyer drafting a court complaint, it is a real concern of law students and schol-

---

2. Richard A. Posner, *Goodbye to the Bluebook*, 53 U. Chi. L. Rev. 1343, 1344 (1986).

3. Bacchus, *supra* note 1, at 254.

ars who must avoid plagiarism in their written work. Most American educational institutions take a strict stand against plagiarism, and many students are surprised at how strict these rules can actually be.[4] This is particularly true for law students in Illinois, because in 1982 the Illinois Supreme Court censured a law student in a graduate program who knowingly plagiarized from two published works. The court stated:

> The extent of the respondent's plagiarism displays an extreme cynicism towards the property rights of others. He incorporated verbatim the work of other authors as a substantial portion of his thesis and obtained no permission for this use. Moreover, this conduct amounted to at least a technical infringement of the publishers' federally protected copyrights. This fraudulent conversion of other people's property is similar to conduct that Illinois and other States have held warrants discipline. [Citations omitted].
>
> The purpose for which respondent used the appropriated material also displays a lack of honesty which cannot go undisciplined, especially because honesty is so fundamental to the functioning of the legal profession.[5]

It did not matter to the Illinois Supreme Court that the author had "an impeccable reputation in the community" or that he had represented "thousands of clients" without complaints from any of them. The court stated:

> All honest scholars are the real victims in this case. The respondent's plagiarism showed disrespect for their legitimate pursuits. Moreover, the respondent's conduct undermined the honor system that is maintained in all institutions of learning. These harms, however, are rather diffuse, and in any event, Northwestern University has already rectified them by expelling the respondent, an act which will

---

4. Mark E. Wojcik, *Introduction to Legal English* 279 (2d ed., Intl. L. Inst. 2001).
5. *In re Lamberis*, 443 N.E.2d 549, 551–52 (Ill. 1982).

also undoubtedly ensure that the respondent will be hereafter excluded from the academic world.[6]

The Illinois Supreme Court decided to censure the attorney. A dissenting opinion thought that a censure was too lenient, however, and urged instead a three-month suspension from the practice of law.[7]

The lesson is this: You must acknowledge the direct use of another person's words. You must acknowledge sources even if you paraphrase the original text. You must also acknowledge the direct use of another person's idea. Proper citations to authority avoid potential problems of plagiarism.

E. Promote Concise Writing

Effective citations allow writers to draft concise sentences because a correct legal citation can convey a great deal of information to a trained reader.[8] A proper citation will "economize on space and the reader's time."[9] For example, a citation to a case in Ill. 2d will tell me that the case was decided by the Illinois Supreme Court. The same is true if the abbreviation "Ill." appears in the parenthetical with the year of the court's decision.

This allows me to cut out words that are "obvious" from the citation.

> For example, consider the following 41-word sentence and its citation:
>
> In Illinois, the Second District of the Illinois Appellate Court ruled in 1994 in the case of *Vann v. Vehrs* that the person who breaks a wedding engagement must return any gifts given in contemplation of marriage, including an en-

---

6. *Id.* at 552.
7. *Id.* at 553 (Underwood, J., dissenting).
8. *See generally* Mark E. Wojcik, *Introduction to Legal English* 283–86 (2d ed., Intl. L. Inst. Institute 2001).
9. Posner, *supra* note 2, at 1344.

gagement ring. *Vann v. Vehrs,* 633 N.E.2d 102, 105 (Ill. App. 2d Dist. 1994).

If we remove the information that is obvious from the citation, the sentence drops from 41 words to 22 words:

> In Illinois, the person who breaks a wedding engagement must return any gifts given in contemplation of marriage, including an engagement ring. *Vann v. Vehrs,* 633 N.E.2d 102, 105 (Ill. App. 2d Dist. 1994).

As some courts now limit briefs to a certain number of words rather than a certain number of pages, the number of words saved in this revised sentence alone suggests that writers should learn to use citations effectively.

F. Show Subsequent Legal History

A citation can tell readers the subsequent legal history of a case, such as whether a case has been affirmed or reversed. For example:

> *Schmidt v. Ottawa Med. Ctr.,*155 F. Supp. 2d 919 (N.D. Ill. 2001), *aff'd,* 322 F.3d 461 (7th Cir. 2003).

II. Citation Manuals

A. The Bluebook

Historically, most legal scholars and professionals followed the citation format of *The Bluebook: A Uniform System of Citation.*[10] It began in 1926 as a 26-page pamphlet for use at Harvard Law School.[11] Seventeen editions later it is 393 pages long. This manual, while useful, is widely criticized because it is difficult to understand

---

10. Editors of the Columbia Law Review *et al., The Bluebook: A Uniform System of Citation* (17th ed., Harvard Law Rev. Assn. 2000).

11. *See e.g.* Bacchus, *supra* note 1, at 250.

and use.[12] Maureen Collins aptly summarized the feelings of many professors, practitioners, and students when she wrote: "I hate the Bluebook. I view it as a necessary evil in a cruel world."[13] And Andrea Kaufman correctly summarized the feelings of many legal research professors when she wrote: "*Bluebook* questions are a teacher's worst enemy because they are impossible to answer intelligently."[14]

Why is *The Bluebook* difficult to use? For one thing, *The Bluebook* gives different citation formats for law review footnotes and for citations in briefs and memoranda. Examples of citations in *The Bluebook* are given for law review footnotes, even though most users of the book were instead writing legal memoranda and briefs. Users of the book had to use the inside front cover of the book convert all of the examples in *The Bluebook* to examples of citations formats for the documents they were writing. Additionally, the book was written by law students who had little understanding of the practice needs and realities of practice. Finally, the book was published in a new edition approximately every five years, and so changes were made without explanation or need. Because the previous group of student authors had graduated from law school, each new edition of the book seemed to have been written by a new group of students entirely unconnected to the previous edition.

Despite these difficulties, generations of lawyers in the United States used *The Bluebook*. It was also used far beyond the United States. For example, I was invited by the Chief Justice of the Supreme Court of India to present a paper at a law conference in New Delhi. The conference organizers asked specifically that citations in the papers conform to *The Bluebook*. It was a strange request, coming from the other side of the world, but it shows how widely *The Bluebook* was being used.

---

12. *See e.g.* James W. Paulsen, *An Uninformed System of Citation*, 105 Harv. L. Rev. 1780 (1992).

13. Maureen B. Collins, *Bluebook Blues: Changes in the Seventeenth Edition*, 88 Ill. B.J. 663 (2000).

14. Andrea Kaufman, *Uncomplicating the Citation Process*, 87 Ill. B.J. 675, 675 (1999).

Because *The Bluebook* was so difficult to use, several sources were developed to help make it easier. These included a short *User's Guide to the Bluebook*,[15] a *Dictionary of Legal Citations*,[16] and a *Dictionary of Legal Abbreviations*.[17]

B. The University of Chicago Maroon Book

The University of Chicago Law School, expressing its dissatisfaction with *The Bluebook*, created its own "Maroon Book" for legal citation.[18] In introducing the book, Judge Richard Posner of the U.S. Court of Appeals for the Seventh Circuit wrote: "From the city Mrs. O'Leary's cow made famous, where they do things that they just don't do on Broadway, now comes the Citation Manual of the Big Shoulders."[19] Despite this splendid endorsement from Judge Posner, the Maroon Book did not really take off among other law schools.

C. The ALWD Citation Manual

In 2000, the Association of Legal Writing Directors and Darby Dickerson published an alternative to *The Bluebook*. The *ALWD Citation Manual: A Professional System of Citation* was universally praised and quickly adopted by law schools and law journals across

---

15. Alan L. Dworsky, *User's Guide to the Bluebook* (William S. Hein & Co. 2002).
16. Mary Miles Prince, *Bieber's Dictionary of Legal Citations*, (5th ed., William S. Hein & Co. 1997).
17. Mary Miles Prince, *Bieber's Dictionary of Legal Abbreviations*, (5th ed., William S. Hein & Co. 2001).
18. *See* The University of Chicago Law Review & The University of Chicago Legal Forum, *The University of Chicago Manual of Legal Citation*, 53 U. Chi. L. Rev. 1353 (1986). Maroon is the school color for the University of Chicago.
19. Richard Posner, *Book Note: Manual Labor, Chicago Style*, 101 Harv. L. Rev. 1323, 1323 (1988).

the country. It has now been published in a second edition.[20] The book is intelligently designed and easy to use. Citation formats are the same for law review footnotes and for memoranda and briefs, so the examples in the *ALWD Citation Manual* are the examples that writers can use. There are "Fast Format" pages at the beginning of each section to provide examples of correct citation formats. "Sidebars" identify common problems and show how to avoid them. There is also a sample memorandum to show how citations are used in context.

Professionals who have not seen the book expressed concerns that citation formats would not follow *The Bluebook*. Most professionals cannot tell the difference between a citation that follows *The Bluebook* and a citation that follows the *ALWD Citation Manual*. In many cases there is no difference between the citations under both systems.

The Bluebook will still have its uses (such as for international materials, for example), but it is only a matter of time until it is entirely replaced by the *ALWD Citation Manual*.

D. Illinois Citation Rules

One of the important features of the *ALWD Citation Manual* is its inclusion of the state-specific citation rules. These are the rules that the state courts require for citations in briefs and memoranda filed in court.

Rule 6 of the Illinois Supreme Court Rules[21] provides specific rules for citing cases, statutes, and books for documents submitted to the Illinois state courts:

---

20. Association of Legal Writing Directors and Darby Dickerson, *ALWD Citation Manual: A Professional System of Citation* (2d ed., Aspen Publishers 2003). Further information about the book (including any updates to the manual) is available from the Association of Legal Writing Directors at www.alwd.org.
21. *See* Ill. Sup. Ct. R. 6 (adopted effective Jan. 20, 1993). The format of the rule has been revised here by breaking it into paragraphs and adding subheadings.

1. *Illinois Cases.* Citations of cases must be by title, to the page of the volume where the case begins, and to the pages upon which the pertinent matter appears in at least one of the reporters cited. It is not sufficient to use only *supra* or *infra*.

    Citation of Illinois cases shall be to the official reports, but the citation to the *North Eastern Reporter* [and] the *Illinois Decisions* may be added. Quotations may be cited from either the official reports or the *North Eastern Reporter* or the *Illinois Decisions.*
2. *Cases From Other Jurisdictions.* Citation of cases from other jurisdictions shall include the date and may be to either the official State reports or the National Reporter System, or both. If only the National Reporter System citation is used, the court rendering the decision shall also be identified.
3. *Textooks.* Textbook citations shall include the date of publication and the edition.
4. *Illinois Statutes.* Illinois statutes shall generally be cited to the *Illinois Compiled Statutes* (ILCS) but citations to the session laws of Illinois shall be made when appropriate. Prior to January 1, 1997, statutory citations may be made to the *Illinois Revised Statutes* instead of or in addition to the *Illinois Compiled Statutes.*

III. Samples of Specific Citations

Many case reporters, treatises, and law journals include notations on how a particular source should be cited. Novice researchers are often thrilled to see such a notation, and once they see it they forgo checking the correct citation format in the citation system they are using (*ALWD* or *Bluebook*). More often than not, the suggested citation will not conform to the citation system being used. The suggested citation may provide a starting point, but the reader should make any necessary adjustments to conform to the *ALWD Citation Manual* or to *The Bluebook.*

Although the rules of citation may differ slightly from system to system, you will be able to master the fundamentals of the system that you use.[22] And no matter which citation system you use, you must be sure that the information in your citation must be accurate. A reader cannot find the case you cite if you have the wrong volume number, reporter series, or page number. And because it cannot be emphasized enough, you must again be sure that you have updated the authorities you cite.

The examples given here first show sample citations in three formats. The first column uses the *ALWD* citation format. This format is the same for briefs, memoranda, and law review articles. The second column used the *Bluebook* citation format for briefs and memoranda. The third column uses the *Bluebook* citation format for law review footnotes. You will note in the third column for law review footnotes that case names are no longer italicized and that publications use LARGE AND SMALL CAPITAL LETTERS. The *Bluebook's* meaningless and aggravating distinction between citation formats for footnotes in law review articles and footnotes in law office memoranda or briefs is a holdover from a pre-computer era when law offices lacked access to the fonts previously used only by professional printers.

Sample Citations

In the following examples, ALWD indicates a sample citation following the *ALWD Citation Manual*, 2d edition; BP indicates a citation in the style of *The Bluebook*, 17th edition (practitioner's format for memoranda and briefs); and BLR indicates a citation in the style of *The Bluebook*, 17th edition (format for law review footnotes).

---

22. You may even be using another citation system not described here, such as the Universal Citation Guide from the American Association of Law Libraries (AALL). The AALL is located at 53 W. Jackson, Suite 940, Chicago, IL 60604. Further information about its universal citation guide is available on its website at http://www.aallnet.org/committee/citation/.

Legal Citation • 187

U.S. Constitution
ALWD U.S. Const. art. I, §1.
BP   U.S. Const. art. I, §1.
BLR   U.S. CONST. art. I, §1.

Illinois Constitution of 1970
ALWD Ill. Const. art. I, §12.
BP   Ill. Const. art. I, §12.
BLR   ILL. CONST. art. I, §12.

U.S. Supreme Court
ALWD *U.S. v. Cleveland Indians Baseball Co.*, 532 U.S. 200 (2001).
BP   *United States v. Cleveland Indians Baseball Co.*, 532 U.S. 200 (2001).
BLR   United States v. Cleveland Indians Baseball Co., 532 U.S. 200 (2001).

U.S. Court of Appeals for the Seventh Circuit
ALWD *ISI Intl. Inc. v. Borden Ladner Gervais LLP*, 316 F.3d 731 (7th Cir. 2003).
BP   *ISI Int'l Inc. v. Borden Ladner Gervais LLP*, 316 F.3d 731 (7th Cir. 2003).
BLR   ISI Int'l Inc. v. Borden Ladner Gervais LLP, 316 F.3d 731 (7th Cir. 2003).

U.S. District Court for the Northern District of Illinois
ALWD *Builders Assn. of Greater Chicago v. City of Chicago*, 240 F. Supp. 2d 796 (N.D. Ill. 2003).
BP   *Builders Ass'n of Greater Chicago v. City of Chicago*, 240 F. Supp. 2d 796 (N.D. Ill. 2003).
BLR   Builders Ass'n of Greater Chicago v. City of Chicago, 240 F. Supp. 2d 796 (N.D. Ill. 2003).

U.S. District Court for the Central District of Illinois
ALWD *U.S. v. White*, 241 F. Supp. 2d 902 (C.D. Ill. 2002).
BP   *United States v. White*, 241 F. Supp. 2d 902 (C.D. Ill. 2002).
BLR   United States v. White, 241 F. Supp. 2d 902 (C.D. Ill. 2002).

U.S. District Court for the Southern District of Illinois
ALWD *Berger v. Xerox Ret. Income Guar. Plan*, 231 F. Supp. 804 (S.D. Ill. 2002).

BP   *Berger v. Xerox Ret. Income Guar. Plan*, 231 F. Supp. 804 (S.D. Ill. 2002).
BLR   Berger v. Xerox Ret. Income Guar. Plan, 231 F. Supp. 804 (S.D. Ill. 2002).

Illinois Supreme Court (not using local rule)
ALWD   *People v. Belk*, 784 N.E.2d 825 (Ill. 2003).
BP   *People v. Belk*, 784 N.E.2d 825 (Ill. 2003).
BLR   People v. Belk, 784 N.E.2d 825 (Ill. 2003).

Illinois Supreme Court (including parallel citations)
ALWD   *People v. Belk*, 203 Ill. 2d 187, 271 Ill. Dec. 271, 784 N.E.2d 825 (2003).
BP   *People v. Belk*, 203 Ill. 2d 187, 271 Ill. Dec. 271, 784 N.E.2d 825 (2003).
BLR   People v. Belk, 203 Ill. 2d 187, 271 Ill. Dec. 271, 784 N.E.2d 825 (2003).

Illinois Appellate Court – First District (not using local rule)
ALWD   *Yates v. Schackelford*, 784 N.E.2d 330 (Ill. App. 1st Dist. 2002).
BP   *Yates v. Schackelford*, 784 N.E.2d 330 (Ill. App. Ct. 2002).
BLR   Yates v. Schackelford, 784 N.E.2d 330 (Ill. App. Ct. 2002).

Illinois Appellate Court – First District (including parallel citations)
ALWD   *Yates v. Schackelford*, 336 Ill. App. 3d 796, 271 Ill. Dec. 112, 784 N.E.2d 330 (1st Dist. 2002).
BP   *Yates v. Schackelford*, 336 Ill. App. 3d 796, 271 Ill. Dec. 112, 784 N.E.2d 330 (2002).
BLR   Yates v. Schackelford, 336 Ill. App. 3d 796, 271 Ill. Dec. 112, 784 N.E.2d 330 (2002).

Illinois Appellate Court – Second District (not using local rule)
ALWD   *Village of Sleepy Hollow v. Pulte Home Corp.*, 783 N.E.2d 1093 (Ill. App. 2d Dist. 2003).
BP   *Village of Sleepy Hollow v. Pulte Home Corp.*, 783 N.E.2d 1093 (Ill. App. Ct. 2003).
BLR   Village of Sleepy Hollow v. Pulte Home Corp., 783 N.E.2d 1093 (Ill. App. Ct. 2003).

Legal Citation • 189

Illinois Appellate Court – Third District (not using local rule)
ALWD People v. Rish, 784 N.E.2d 889 (Ill. App. 3d Dist. 2003).
BP   People v. Rish, 784 N.E.2d 889 (Ill. App. Ct. 2003).
BLR   People v. Rish, 784 N.E.2d 889 (Ill. App. Ct. 2003).

Illinois Appellate Court – Fourth District (not using local rule)
ALWD Long v. Mathew, 783 N.E.2d 1076 (Ill. App. 4th Dist. 2003).
BP   Long v. Mathew, 783 N.E.2d 1076 (Ill. App. Ct. 2003).
BLR   Long v. Mathew, 783 N.E.2d 1076 (Ill. App. Ct. 2003).

Illinois Appellate Court – Fifth District (not using local rule)
ALWD Jines v. Jurich, 783 N.E.2d 147 (Ill. App. 5th Dist. 2002).
BP   *Jines v. Jurich*, 783 N.E.2d 147 (Ill. App. Ct. 2002).
BLR   Jines v. Jurich, 783 N.E.2d 147 (Ill. App. Ct. 2002).

Illinois Supreme Court Rule
ALWD Ill. S. Ct. R. 715
BP   Ill. S. Ct. R. 715
BLR   Ill. S. Ct. R. 715

Illinois Compiled Statutes (Official Version)[23]
See Footnote

Illinois Compiled Statutes, State Bar Association Edition
ALWD 720 Ill. Comp. Stat. 5/16B-2 (West 2001).
BP   720 Ill. Comp. Stat. 5/16B-2 (West 2001).
BLR   720 Ill. Comp. Stat. 5/16B-2 (West 2001).

Illinois Compiled Statutes Annotated (LexisNexis)
ALWD 720 Ill. Comp. Stat. Ann. 5/16B-2 (LexisNexis 2002).
BP   720 Ill. Comp. Stat. Ann. 5/16B-2 (LexisNexis 2002).
BLR   720 Ill. Comp. Stat. Ann. 5/16B-2 (LexisNexis 2002).

---

23. Although the *ALWD Citation Manual* and the *Bluebook* both suggest that there is an official version of the Illinois Compiled Statutes, there is no official version of the Illinois statutes in print, CD-ROM, or on the Internet. The "State Bar Association Edition" is not an official version, it is only an unannotated version. Researchers should accordingly cite one of the three non-official versions: the State Bar Association Edition, the annotated version published by LexisNexis, or the annotated version published by West.

West's Smith-Hurd Illinois Compiled Statutes Annotated (West)
ALWD 720 Ill. Comp. Stat. Ann. 5/16B-2 (West 2002).
BP   720 Ill. Comp. Stat. Ann. 5/16B-2 (West 2002).
BLR   720 Ill. Comp. Stat. Ann. 5/16B-2 (West 2002).

Session Law
ALWD 2001 Ill. Laws 3449
BP   2001 Ill. Laws 3449
BLR   2001 Ill. Laws 3449

Illinois Legislative Service
ALWD 2003 Ill. Legis. Serv. 2684 (West)
BP   2003 Ill. Legis. Serv. 2684 (West)
BLR   2003 Ill. Legis. Serv. 2684 (West)

Illinois Administrative Code[24]
ALWD Ill. Admin. Code tit. 77, pt. 250 (1996).
BP   Ill. Admin. Code tit. 77, pt. 250 (1996).
BLR   Ill. Admin. Code tit. 77, pt. 250 (1996).

Illinois Register
ALWD 27 Ill. Register 5068 (Mar. 28, 2003).
BP   27 Ill. Reg. 5068 (Mar. 28, 2003).
BLR   27 Ill. Reg. 5068 (Mar. 28, 2003).

Illinois Court of Claims
ALWD *Rubidoux v. Northeastern Ill. U.*, 51 Ill. Cl. 275 (1998).
BP   *Rubidoux v. Northeastern Ill. Univ.*, 51 Ill. Ct. Cl. 275 (1998).
BLR   Rubidoux v. Northeastern Ill. Univ., 51 Ill. Ct. Cl. 275 (1998).

---

24. Illinois regulations are often difficult to cite because they are difficult to find. As explained in the chapter on Administrative Law, the Illinois regulations last appeared in print in 1996, and current print versions merely reprint that version and supplement it with excerpts from the *Illinois Register*. If the Illinois regulations are again published in print, a better way to cite them may be to refer to specific section numbers rather than parts. For example, a future citation may look like this: 77 Ill. Admin. Code § 250.140 (2006).

Illinois Courts Commission
- ALWD *In re O'Brien,* 3 Ill. Cts. Commn. 85 (1995).
- BP *In re O'Brien,* 3 Ill. Cts. Comm'n 85 (1995).
- BLR In re O'Brien, 3 Ill. Cts. Comm'n 85 (1995).

Treatise
- ALWD John E. Corkery, *Illinois Civil and Criminal Evidence* § 501.304 (L. Bull. Publg. Co. 2000).
- BP John E. Corkery, *Illinois Civil and Criminal Evidence* § 501.304 (2000).
- BLR John E. Corkery, Illinois Civil and Criminal Evidence § 501.304 (2000).

Illinois Jurisprudence (State Legal Encyclopedia)
- ALWD Thomas Curry, Joseph V. Collina, & Theresa Whitely, *Criminal Law and Procedure,* Ill. Jur. Vol. 1, § 1:14, at 25 (LexisNexis 2002).
- BP Thomas Curry, Joseph V. Collina, & Theresa Whitely, *Criminal Law and Procedure,* 1 Ill. Jur. § 1:14, at 25 (2002).
- BLR Thomas Curry, Joseph V. Collina, & Theresa Whitely, *Criminal Law and Procedure,* 1 Ill. Jur. § 1:14, at 25 (2002).

Illinois Law and Practice (State Legal Encyclopedia)
- ALWD Paul Coltoff, Stephen Lease, & Thomas Muskus, *Criminal Law,* 14B Ill. L. & Prac. vol. 14B, §464, at 72 (West Group 1999).
- BP Paul Coltoff, Stephen Lease, & Thomas Muskus, *Criminal Law,* 14B Ill. L. & Prac. §464, at 72 (1999).
- BLR Paul Coltoff, Stephen Lease, & Thomas Muskus, *Criminal Law,* 14B Ill. L. & Prac. §464, at 72 (1999).

Law Review Article
- ALWD Mark E. Wojcik, *Lawyers Who Lie On-Line: How Should the Legal Profession Respond to eBay Ethics?,* 18 J. Marshall J. Computer & Info. L. 875 (2000).
- BP Mark E. Wojcik, *Lawyers Who Lie On-Line: How Should the Legal Profession Respond to eBay Ethics?,* 18 J. Marshall J. Computer & Info. L. 875 (2000).

BLR Mark E. Wojcik, *Lawyers Who Lie On-Line: How Should the Legal Profession Respond to eBay Ethics?*, 18 J. MARSHALL J. COMPUTER & INFO. L. 875 (2000).

Law Review Article by a Student Author

ALWD Ernesto Palomo, Student Author, "*The Sheriff Knows Who the Troublemakers Are. Just Let Him Round Them Up*": *Chicago's New Gang Loitering Ordinance*, 2002 U. Ill. L. Rev. 729.

BP Ernesto Palomo, Comment, "*The Sheriff Knows Who the Troublemakers Are. Just Let Him Round Them Up*": *Chicago's New Gang Loitering Ordinance*, 2002 U. Ill. L. Rev. 729.

BLR Ernesto Palomo, Comment, "*The Sheriff Knows Who the Troublemakers Are. Just Let Him Round Them Up*": *Chicago's New Gang Loitering Ordinance*, 2002 U. ILL. L. REV. 729.

Restatement

ALWD *Restatement (Third) of the Law Governing Lawyers* §38 (2000).

BP *Restatement (Third) of the Law Governing Lawyers* §38 (2000).

BLR RESTATEMENT (THIRD) OF THE LAW GOVERNING LAWYERS §38 (2000).

A.L.R. Annotation

ALWD George L. Blum, *Falsehoods, Misrepresentations, Impersonations, and Other Irresponsible Conduct as Bearing on Requisite Good Moral Character for Admission to the Bar—Conduct Related to Admission to Bar*, 107 A.L.R.5th 167 (2003).

BP George L. Blum, Annotation, *Falsehoods, Misrepresentations, Impersonations, and Other Irresponsible Conduct as Bearing on Requisite Good Moral Character for Admission to the Bar—Conduct Related to Admission to Bar*, 107 A.L.R.5th 167 (2003).

BLR George L. Blum, Annotation, *Falsehoods, Misrepresentations, Impersonations, and Other Irresponsible Conduct as Bearing on Requisite Good Moral Character for Admission to the Bar—Conduct Related to Admission to Bar,* 107 A.L.R.5th 167 (2003).

Additional Resources

Association of Legal Writing Directors & Darby Dickerson, *ALWD Citation Manual: A Professional System of Citation* (2d ed., Aspen Publishers 2003).

Collins, Maureen B. *Bluebook Blues: Changes in the Seventeenth Edition,* 88 Ill. B.J. 663 (2000).

Dworsky, Alan L. *User's Guide to the Bluebook* (William S. Hein & Co. 2002).

Editors of the Columbia Law Review et al., *The Bluebook: A Uniform System of Citation* (17th ed., Harvard Law Rev. Assn. 2000).

Grantmore, Gil. *The Death of Contra,* 52 Stan. L. Rev. 889 (2000).

Hurt, Christine. *Network Effects and Legal Citation: How Antitrust Theory Predicts Who Will Build a Better Bluebook Mousetrap in the Age of Electronic Mice,* 87 Iowa L. Rev. 1257 (2002).

Kaufman, Andrea. *Uncomplicating the Citation Process,* 87 Ill. B.J. 675 (1999).

LeFave, Wayne R. *Livreblue 17: Les Conséquences Tragiques Forgée par le Professeur Répugnant Nommé Grantmore,* 2001 U. Ill. L. Rev. 857.

Posner, Richard A. *Goodbye to the Bluebook,* 53 U. Chi. L. Rev. 1343 (1986).

Prince, Mary Miles. *Bieber's Dictionary of Legal Abbreviations* (5th ed., William S. Hein & Co. 2001).

Prince, Mary Miles. *Bieber's Dictionary of Legal Citations* (5th ed., William S. Hein & Co. 1997).

Wojcik, Mark E. *Introduction to Legal English: An Introduction to Legal Terminology, Reasoning, and Writing in Plain English* 273–90 (2d ed., Intl. L. Inst. 2001).

Chapter 12

Electronic Legal Research

Many legal materials are available on-line, including cases, statutes, regulations, public records, and secondary sources. Court dockets, forms, and images of filed documents are available in many federal courts as a result of the E-Government Act of 2002.[1] State courts are not as far along as the federal courts, but they are continuing to make progress in providing this information. A list of websites for federal and state courts in Illinois follows this chapter in Appendix A, and much information can be found there. Appendix B includes the website addresses of 50 state government offices where additional information and resources can be found.

Electronic research has changed the nature of legal research itself, and it is now as common to do legal research on-line as it is to use books. Some research needs, such as updating authorities, are undoubtedly best accomplished with the electronic versions of Shepard's on LexisNexis and with KeyCite on Westlaw. These services include training resources such as reference materials, tutorials, and classes.

Fee-based databases such as LexisNexis and Westlaw have recently found themselves challenged by many free services available on the Internet. FindLaw, for example, has a great collection of state materials.[2] At the present time, the Internet is not a complete substitute for more reliable databases. It is, however, "a quick and inexpensive

---

1. 44 U.S.C. § 3501 (2002); *see* Paul M. Bush, *Online Availability of Case Information*, Natl. L.J., May 5, 2003, at C6.
2. http://www.findlaw.com

way to find recent federal cases, recent Illinois cases, federal government information, and factual information on any subject."[3]

Information from courts and government agencies is generally reliable when found on official websites, and chapters in this book have included references to specific electronic resources. Electronic access to the Library of Congress,[4] the catalog of federal government publications,[5] and to other federal[6] and state[7] government agencies is also incredibly easy on the Internet. For some sources, such as tracking current Illinois legislation, the Illinois General Assembly website is undoubtedly the best source available.[8] You can also use the Internet to locate depository libraries in your area[9] or simply browse federal resources on specific topics.[10]

While the Internet makes many legal materials available quickly and at little or no cost, the materials are often difficult to research because they are largely still in the early stages of indexing.[11] Many databases are also inadvertently incomplete, and there will likely be no disclaimer on many sites that certain materials are not available. Search engines also produce different results, and may miss cases that are important to your research.

There are many opportunities to receive instruction on using Westlaw or LexisNexis. Because the computerized materials and formats change so frequently, this book does not include any specific information on searching Illinois law using either of those fee-based

---

3. James Cameron & Mary Ellen LeBlanc, *Introduction and Technical Basics 3*, in *The Internet Guide for Illinois Lawyers* (Marry Ellen LeBlanc & John M. Rossi, eds., Ill. Inst. for CLE 1997).
4. http://thomas.loc.gov
5. See http://www.gpo.gov/gpoaccess/locators/cgp or http:///www.gpo.gov/gpoaccess/locators/agency
6. http://www.gpo.gov/gpoaccess/locators/search
7. See Appendix B.
8. http://www.legis.state.il.us/
9. http://www.gpo.gov/gpoaccess/locators/findlibs
10. http://www.gpo.gov/gpoaccess/locators/topics
11. Steven D. Imparl, *Internet Law – The Complete Guide* ch. III, at 1–19 (Specialty Technical Publishers 1998).

computerized services. Information on searching Illinois law will be part of the training course, or you can contact the research support numbers for either service.

You may be learning legal research in a school that prohibits you from using the Internet or a computer-based research service such as Westlaw or LexisNexis, at least in your first semester. You may wonder about the wisdom of such a measure that seems to deny the existence and usefulness of electronic legal research. There has been, and will continue to be, considerable debate about the best pedagogy for teaching legal research. If you find yourself in a situation where you are prohibited from using electronic sources in your first semester, keep in mind that the semester will pass more quickly than you may think, and that this is your opportunity to learn how to use the print sources effectively. If you learn and understand the print sources first, you will be able to use the electronic sources more effectively when doing research for your clients.

Don't confuse "search" with "research." Even if you are able to find sources quickly, do not sacrifice the time you need to analyze those sources, draw analogies where there is no direct support, and to carefully apply the facts to the rules of law that you find.

The Internet is a valuable tool. But when you use the Internet to supplement your other research, you should have a clear idea of your research strategy. If you don't, you will find that you are spending a lot of time surfing the Internet without necessarily finding the information that you need.

Additional Resources

Baugher, Peter V. *The Northern District of Illinois on the World Wide Web,* 16 CBA Rec. 30 (Jan. 2002).

Bush, Paul M. *Online Availability of Case Information,* Natl. L.J., May 5, 2003, at C6.

Callister, Paul D. *Legal Research and the Ballad of John Henry,* 91 Ill. B.J. 261 (2003).

Collins, Maureen B. *E-mail and Attorney Client Communications,* 88 Ill. B.J. 541 (2000).

Cunningham, Thomas J. *Stop Surfing and Get Back to Work: Productive Net Use for Attorneys,* 11 CBA Rec. 28 (Sept. 1997).

Duggan, James E. *Internet Update: Cases and Illinois Statutes,* 87 Ill. B.J. 501 (1999).

Flaming, Todd H. *The Internet is Growing Up,* 86 Ill. B.J. 341 (1998).

French, Thomas R. *Internet Resources for Researching International and Foreign Law,* 52 Syracuse L. Rev. 1167 (2002).

Holynski, Thaddeus J. *Legal Research on the World Wide Web,* 52 Syracuse L. Rev. 1141 (2002).

Hook, Peter A. *Law Librarians Can Help You Save Money and Do Better Research,* 90 Ill. B.J. 373 (July 2002).

Imparl, Steven D. *Internet Law – The Complete Guide* III 1–19 (1998).

LeBlanc, Mary Ellen & John M. Rossi, eds., *The Internet Guide for Illinois Lawyers* (Ill. Inst. for CLE 1997).

Levitt, Carole. *How to Use the Internet for Legal, Business, and Investigative Research: A Guide for Legal Professionals* (5th ed., Internet for Lawyers 2002).

Mays, Antje. *Legal Research on the Internet – A Compendium of Websites to Access United States Federal, State, Local, and International Laws* (William S. Hein & Co. 1999) (Volume 33 of the Legal Research Guide Series).

Olmi, Adria P. *Must-Have Bookmarks: The Cornell Law Library and the Legal Information Institute,* 89 Ill. B.J. 153 (2001).

Olmi, Adria P. *Real-Estate Resources on the Internet for Illinois Lawyers,* 89 Ill. B.J. 495 (2001).

Olmi, Adria P. *Family-Law Resources on the Internet for Illinois Lawyers,* 89 Ill. B.J. 603 (2001).

Olmi, Adria P. *Litigation Resources on the 'Net for Illinois Lawyers*, 90 Ill. B.J. 381 (2002).

Olmi, Adria P. *Internet Research for Illinois Corporate and Securities Lawyers*, 90 Ill. B.J. 267 (2002).

Olmi, Adria P. *Internet Resources for Illinois Personal Injury Lawyers*, 90 Ill. B.J. 151 (2002).

Olmi, Adria P. *Treasure Hunting at State Agency Web Sites*, 89 Ill. B.J. 333 (2001).

Roberge, Linda, Susan B. Long, and David B. Burnham. *Data Warehouses and Data Mining Tools for the Legal Profession: Using Information Technology to Raise the Standard of Practice*, 52 Syracuse L. Rev. 1281 (2002).

Roznavschi, Mirela. *Toward a Cyberlegal Culture: Legal Research on the Frontier of Innovation* (2d ed., Transnational Legal Publishers 2002).

Scott, Wendy. *Evaluating and Authenticating Legal Web Resources: A Practical Guide for Attorneys*, 52 Syracuse L. Rev. 1185 (2002).

Serfass, Melissa M. & Jessie L. Cranford, *Loislaw User's Guide* (Aspen Publishers 2002).

Smith-Butler, Lisa. *Cost Effective Legal Research*, 18(2) Legal Reference Services Q. 61 (2000).

Wendt, Laurel. *Illinois Legal Research Manual* 215–18 (Butterworth Legal Publishers 1988).

Appendix A

Website Addresses for Illinois Courts

These websites contain forms, court rules, and general information about the courts. Website addresses and information on the websites are, of course, subject to frequent change.

Federal Courts

U.S. Court of Appeals for the Seventh Circuit
http://www.ca7.uscourts.gov/

U.S. District Court for the Northern District of Illinois
http://www.ilnd.uscourts.gov/

U.S. District Court for Central District of Illinois
http://www.ilcd.uscourts.gov/

U.S. District Court for Southern District of Illinois
http://www.ilsd.uscourts.gov/

U.S. Bankruptcy Court for the Northern District of Illinois
http://www.ilnb.uscourts.gov/

U.S. Bankruptcy Court for the Central District of Illinois
http://www.ilcb.uscourts.gov/

U.S. Bankruptcy Court for the Southern District of Illinois
http://www.ilsb.uscourts.gov/

State Courts

Illinois Supreme Court
http://www.state.il.us/court/SupremeCourt/

Illinois Appellate Court
http://www.state.il.us/court/AppellateCourt/

Circuit Court of Cook County
http://www.cookcountycourt.org

First Judicial Circuit (Alexander, Jackson, Johnson, Massac, Pope, Pulaski, Saline, Union, Williamson Counties)
http://www.circuitclerk.co.jackson.il.us

Fourth Judicial Circuit (Christian, Clay, Clinton, Effingham, Fayette, Jasper, Marion, Montgomery, and Shelby Counties)
http://www.effingham.net/4thcircuit

Sixth Judicial Circuit (Champaign, DeWitt, Douglas, Macon, Moultrie, and Platt Counties)
http://court.co.macon.il.us/Home.htm

Seventh Judicial Circuit (Greene, Jersey, Macoupin, Morgan, and Sangamon Counties)
http://www.co.sangamon.il.us/Court

Eighth Judicial Circuit (Adams, Brown, Calhoun, Cass, Mason, Menard, Pike, and Schuyler Counties)
http://www.co.adams.il.us/courts/index.htm

Eleventh Judicial Circuit (Ford, Livingston, Logan, McLean, and Woodford Counties)
http://www.mclean.gov/circuitcourt

Fifteenth Judicial Circuit (Carroll, Jo Daviess, Lee, Ogle, and Stephenson Counties)
http://jodaviess.org

Sixteenth Judicial Circuit (DeKalb, Kane and Kendall Counties)
http://www.co.kane.il.us/judicial/index.htm

Seventeenth Judicial Circuit (Boone and Winnebago Counties)
http://www.co.winnebago.il.us/trialct/main.html

Eighteenth Judicial Circuit (DuPage County)
http://www.co.dupage.il.us/courtclerk/index.html

Nineteenth Judicial Circuit (Lake and McHenry Counties)
http://www.19thcircuitcourt.state.il.us

Twenty-first Judicial Circuit (Iroquois and Kankakee Counties)
http://www.prairienet.org/fordiroq/21st/21st.htm

Appendix B

Selected Constitutional Offices, Administrative Agencies, and Special Government Commissions and Committees for the State of Illinois

1. Office of the Governor of Illinois
   207 State House
   Springfield, IL 62706
   217-782-0244
   Website: www.state.il.us/gov/
2. Office of the Lieutenant Governor of Illinois
   214 State House
   Springfield, IL 62706
   217-782-7884
   Website: www.state.il.us/ltgov
3. Office of the Illinois Attorney General
   100 W. Randolph Street
   Chicago, IL 60601
   312-814-3000
   or
   500 S. Second Street
   Springfield, IL 62706
   217-782-1090
   Website: www.ag.state.il.us/toc.htm

4. Illinois Secretary of State
   213 State Capitol
   Springfield, IL 62706
   800-252-8980
   Website: www.sos.state.il.us/
5. Illinois Comptroller
   201 State Capitol
   Springfield, IL 62706-0001
   217-782-6000
   Website: www.ioc.state.il.us/
6. Illinois State Treasurer
   100 W. Randolph Street, Suite 15-600
   Chicago, IL 60601
   312-814-1700
   or
   219 State House
   Springfield, IL 62706
   217-782-2211
   Website: www.state.il.us/treas
7. Illinois Department on Aging
   100 W. Randolph Street, Suite 10-350
   Chicago, IL 60601
   312-814-2630
   or
   421 E. Capitol Ave., Room 100
   Springfield, IL 62701-1789
   217-785-3356
   Website: www.state.il.us/aging/
8. Illinois Department of Agriculture
   100 W. Randolph Street, Suite 10-700
   Chicago, IL 60601
   312-814-6900
   or
   P.O. Box 19281
   Springfield, IL 62794
   217-785-4789
   Website: www.agr.state.il.us/

9. Illinois Department of Children and Family Services (DCFS)
100 W. Randolph, 6th Floor
Chicago, IL 60601
312-814-6800
or
406 Monroe Street
Springfield, IL 62701
217-785-2509
Website:www.state.il.us/defs/index.shtml

10. Illinois Department of Commerce and Economic Opportunity
100 W. Randolph Street, Suite 3-400
Chicago, IL 60601
312-814-7179
or
620 E. Adams
Springfield, IL 62701
217-782-7500
Website: www.commerce.state.il.us/

11. Illinois Department of Corrections
100 W. Randolph Street, Suite 4-200
Chicago, IL 60601
312-814-3017
or
1301 Concordia Ct.
P.O. Box 19277
Springfield, IL 62794
217-522-2666
Website: www.idoc.state.il.us/

12. Illinois Department of Employment Security
401 S. State Street
Chicago, IL 60605
312-793-5700
or
400 W. Monroe Street, Suite 303
Springfield, IL 62704
217-785-5070
Website: www.ides.state.il.us/

13. Illinois Department of Financial Institutions
    100 W. Randolph Street, Suite 15-700
    Chicago, IL 60601
    312-814-2000
    or
    500 Ides Park Place, Suite 510
    Springfield, IL 62718
    217-782-2831
    Website: www.state.il.us/dfi/
14. Illinois Department of Human Rights
    100 W. Randolph Street, Suite 10-100
    Chicago, IL 60601
    312-814-6245
    or
    222 S. College, 1st Floor, Room 101A
    Springfield, IL 62704
    217-785-5100
    Website: www.state.il.us/dhr/
15. Illinois Department of Human Services
    401 S. Clinton Ave., 7th Floor
    Chicago, IL 60607
    800-252-8635
    or
    100 S. Grand Ave, 3rd Floor
    Springfield, IL 62762
    800-483-6154
    Website: www.state.il.us/agency/dhs/
16. Illinois Emergency Management Agency
    110 E. Adams
    Springfield, IL 62701-1109
    217-782-2700
    Website: www.state.il.us/iema/
17. Illinois Environmental Protection Agency
    100 W. Randolph Street, Suite 11-300
    Chicago, IL 60601
    312-814-6026

or
1021 N. Grand Ave.
P.O. Box 19276
Springfield, IL 62794-9276
217-782-3397
Website: www.epa.state.il.us/

18. Illinois Historic Preservation Agency
100 W. Randolph Street, Suite 5-916
Chicago, IL 60601-3103
312-814-1409
or:
1 Old State Capitol
Springfield, IL 62701-1507
217-785-7930
Website: www.state.il.us/HPA/

19. Illinois State Police
100 W. Randolph Street, Suite 4-600
Chicago, IL 60601
312-814-2834
or
103 Armory Building
P.O. Box 19461-9461
Springfield, IL 62794
217-782-7263
Website: www.state.il.us/isp/isphpagen.html

20. Illinois Department of Insurance
100 W. Randolph Street, Suite 15-100
Chicago, IL 60601-3251
312-814-2420
or
320 W. Washington, 4th Floor
Springfield, IL 62767-0001
217-782-4515
Website: www.state.il.us/INS/

21. Illinois Department of Labor
    160 N. LaSalle Street, Room C-1300
    Chicago, IL 60601
    312-793-2800
    or
    1 Old State Capitol Plaza, 3rd Floor
    Springfield, IL 62701
    217-782-6206
    or
    2309 W. Main
    Marion, IL 62959
    618-993-7090
    Website: www.state.il.us/agency/idol

22. Illinois Department of Natural Resources
    100 W. Randolph Street, Suite 4-300
    Chicago, IL 60601
    312-814-2071
    or
    524 S. Second Street
    Springfield, IL 62701-1787
    217-785-0075
    Website: http://dnr.state.il.us/

23. Illinois Department of Nuclear Safety
    1035 Outer Park Dr.
    Springfield, IL 62704
    217-785-9900
    or
    800 Roosevelt Rd., Building C, Suite 200
    Glen Ellyn, IL 60137
    630-790-5300
    Website: www.state.il.us/idns/

24. Illinois Department of Professional Regulation
    100 W. Randolph Street, Suite 9-300
    Chicago, IL 60601
    312-814-4500
    or

320 W. Washington, 3rd Floor
Springfield, IL 62786
217-785-0800
Website: www.dpr.state.il.us/

25. Illinois Department of Public Aid
401 Clinton Ave.
Chicago, IL 60607
312-793-4792
or
201 S. Grand Ave.
Springfield, IL 62763
217-782-1200
Website: www.state.il.us/dpa/

26. Illinois Department of Public Health
100 W. Randolph Street, Suite C-600
Chicago, IL 60601
312-814-2608
or
535 W. Jefferson Street
Springfield, IL 62761
217-782-4977
Website: www.idph.state.il.us/

27. Illinois Department of Revenue
100 W. Randolph, Suite 7-500
Chicago, IL 60601
312-814-5270
or
101 W. Jefferson Street
Springfield, IL 62794
217-785-2602
Website: www.revenue.state.il.us/

28. Illinois Department of Transportation
310 S. Michigan Ave., Room 1600
Chicago, IL 60604
312-793-2250
or

2300 S. Dirksen Parkway
Springfield, IL 62764
217-782-5597
Website: www.dot.state.il.us/

29. Illinois Department of Veterans' Affairs
100 W. Randolph, Suite 4-650
Chicago, IL 60601
312-814-2460
or
833 S. Spring Street
P.O. Box 19432
Springfield, IL 62794
217-782-6641
800-437-9824
Website: www.state.il.us/agency/DVA

30. Illinois Commerce Commission
160 N. LaSalle Street, Suite C-800
Chicago, IL 60601
312-814-2859
or
527 E. Capitol Ave.
Springfield, IL 62794
217-782-7907
Website: www.icc.state.il.us/

31. Illinois State Board of Elections
100 W. Randolph, Suite 14-100
Chicago, IL 60601
312-814-6440
or
1020 S. Spring
P.O. Box 4187
Springfield, IL 627048
217-782-4141
Website: www.elections.state.il.us/

32. Illinois Office of Banks and Real Estate
    310 S. Michigan Ave., Suite 2130
    Chicago, IL 60604-4278
    312-793-3000
    or
    500 E. Monroe Street
    Springfield, IL 62701
    217-782-3000
    Website: www.obre.state.il.us/
33. Illinois Board of Education
    100 W. Randolph Street, Suite 14-300,
    Chicago, IL 60601
    312-814-2220
    or
    100 N. First Street, Room S-404
    Springfield, IL 62777
    217-782-9560
    Website: www.isbe.state.il.us/
34. Illinois Board of Higher Education
    4 W. Old Capitol Plaza, Room 500
    Springfield, IL 62701
    217-782-2551
    Website: www.ibhe.state.il.us/
35. Occupational Information Coordinating Committee
    217 E. Monroe, Suite 203
    Springfield, IL 62706
    217-785-0789
    Website: www.ioicc.state.il.us/
36. Illinois Pollution Control Board
    100 W. Randolph Street, Suite 11-500
    Chicago, IL 60601
    312-814-3620
    or
    600 S. Second, Suite 402
    Springfield, IL 62704
    217-524-8500
    Website: www.ipcb.state.il.us/

37. Auditor General
    100 W Randolph Street, Suite 4-100
    Chicago, IL 60601
    312-814-4000
    or
    740 E. Ash Street
    Springfield, IL 62703
    217-782-6046
    Website: www.state.il.us/auditor/
38. Illinois Appellate Defender
    100 W. Randolph Street, Suite 5-500
    Chicago, IL 60601
    312-814-5472
    or
    400 S. Ninth Street, Suite 201
    Springfield, IL 62705
    217-782-7203
    Website: www.state.il.us/defender/
39. Illinois Appellate Prosecutor
    725 S. Second Street
    Springfield, IL 62704
    217-782-1628
    Website: www.state.il.us/prosecutor/
40. Illinois Property Tax Appeal Board
    402 Stratton Bldg.
    Springfield, IL 62706
    217-782-6076
    Website: www.state.il.us/agency/ptab/
41. Illinois Guardianship and Advocacy Commission
    160 N. LaSalle Street, Suite S-500
    Chicago, IL 60601
    312-793-5908
    or
    421 E. Capitol, Suite 205
    Springfield, IL 62701
    Website: www.state.il.us/igac/

42. Illinois Human Rights Commission
100 W. Randolph Street, Suite 5-100
Chicago, IL 60601
312-814-6269
or
404 Stratton Bldg.
Springfield, IL 62706
217-785-4350
Website: www.state.il.us/ihrc
43. Illinois Housing Development Authority
401 N. Michigan Ave., Suite 900
Chicago, IL 60611
312-836-5200
Website: www.ihda.org
44. Illinois Industrial Commission
100 W. Randolph Street, Suite 8-200
Chicago, IL 60601
312-814-6500
or
701 S. Second Street
Springfield, IL 62704
217-785-7087
Website: www.state.il.us/agancy/iic/
45. Illinois Criminal Justice Information Authority
120 S. Riverside Plaza, 10th Floor
Chicago, IL 60606-3997
312-793-8550
Website: www.icjia.state.il.us/public/index.cfm
46. Illinois Liquor Control Commission
100 W. Randolph Street, Suite 5-300
Chicago, IL 60601
312-814-2206
or
222 W. College Street, Room 100
Springfield, IL 62704
217-782-2136
Website: www.state.il.us/lcc/

47. Illinois Building Commission
    420 Stratton Bldg
    Springfield, IL 62706
    217-557-7500
    Website: www.illbc.org

48. Illinois Council on Developmental Disabilities
    100 W. Randolph Street, Suite 10-600
    Chicago, IL 60601
    312-814-2080
    Website: www.state.il.us/agency/ipcdd/

49. Illinois Educational Labor Relations Board
    320 W. Washington Street, 2nd Floor
    Springfield, IL 62701-1135
    217-782-9068
    Website: www.state.il.us/agency/ielrb/

50. Judicial Inquiry Board
    100 W. Randolph Street, Suite 14-500
    Chicago, IL 60601
    312-814-5554
    Website: www.state.il.us/jib

Appendix C

Illinois Legal Research Quiz

1. What is the most overlooked research resource in the library? Please give an example of how you can use this research resource effectively.
2. When researching an area of law that is unfamiliar to you, why might it be helpful to first consult a secondary source?
3. Can you identify some purposes served by legal encyclopedias?
4. Which of the following are primary sources of law? Please circle the letter of each primary source.
   a. A decision from the Illinois Supreme Court
   b. A decision from the United States District Court for the Northern District of Illinois
   c. A decision from the United States Court of Appeals for the Seventh Circuit
   d. A decision from the United States Court of Appeals for the Ninth Circuit
   e. *American Jurisprudence, Second Series*
   f. A law review article by Professor Mark E. Wojcik
   g. Code of Federal Regulations
   h. *Corpus Juris Secundum*
   i. *Federal Digest*
   j. Federal Rules of Appellate Procedure
   k. Federal Rules of Criminal Procedure
   l. Illinois Constitution
   m. Illinois Constitution of 1870
   n. Iowa Constitution
   o. The *Illinois Bar Journal*

p. *Illinois Digest*
q. *Illinois Jurisprudence*
r. *Illinois Law and Practice*
s. Illinois Rules of Civil Procedure
t. Illinois Supreme Court Rules
u. *Restatement (Second) of Torts*
v. Statutes found in the *Illinois Compiled Statutes*
w. Statutes found in the *United States Code*
x. Treaties
y. Treatises
z. U.S. Constitution

5. If you are researching a state law issue, should you generally consult a national legal encyclopedia or a state encyclopedia?

6. What is the difference between primary and secondary authority?

7. What is the difference between binding and persuasive authority?

8. How can you find a law review article?

9. If the research you find on Illinois law does not support a favorable outcome for your client, what can you do?
   a. Refuse to return telephone calls from your client.
   b. Demand a large retainer before doing any further work on the case.
   c. Bury the other side in discovery requests, including interrogatories, requests to produce documents, and requests to admit certain facts.
   d. Tell the client that he or she should take her chance before the jury.
   e. Tell the client that he or she is out of luck.
   f. Advise the client to move to Wisconsin.
   g. Research persuasive authority to see if there might be another approach to the problem, and if not, inform the client that he or she is unlikely to prevail under the current law.

10. While using the *Illinois Digest* to research a state law question, you find a citation to a decision from the United States District Court for the Northern District of Illinois. Will that federal

court decision on an issue of Illinois state law be binding or persuasive on a judge sitting in the Circuit Court of Cook County?

11. What is the role of the executive branch of government?
12. What is the role of the Illinois Attorney General?
13. Where can you find extrinsic evidence of legislative intent, and why would you ever want to?
14. Can the Illinois Supreme Court overrule a decision of the First District of the Illinois Appellate Court?
15. If a party loses at a trial conducted in Cook County, to which district of the Illinois Appellate Court could the losing party appeal?
16. Can the First District of the Illinois Appellate Court overrule a decision of the Illinois Supreme Court?
17. Can the Illinois Supreme Court overrule a decision that it made last year?
18. Is a published decision of the United States Court of Appeals for the Ninth Circuit binding or persuasive on the United States Court of Appeals for the Seventh Circuit?
19. Is a decision from the Nebraska Supreme Court binding or persuasive on the Illinois Supreme Court?
20. If a court is bound by a judicial decision rendered by a higher court, how might the court distinguish that earlier precedent?
21. What is a code?
22. What is the *Illinois Register* and when would you want to look at it?
23. What is a headnote on a judicial decision? Can you quote or otherwise cite a headnote, or must you find the portion of the decision described by the headnote?
24. What is a "parallel cite" for a court decision?
25. What is a digest?
26. To "shepardize" means to update a legal authority using the *Shepard's Citators*. Why would you want to update a legal authority that you are citing in your memorandum or brief?

27. What is a "form book," and why might you want to use one?
28. Is an ISBA Ethics Opinion binding or persuasive on an Illinois court?
29. What is the Illinois Court of Claims, and where can you find its decisions?
30. What states are covered by the U.S. Court of Appeals for the Seventh Circuit?

Index

ALR Annotations 112, 146–47, 192–93
Administrative Code 190
Administrative Office of the Illinois Courts 64
Advance Sheets 63, 72, 121
Agriculture, Department of 206
ALWD Citation Manual xx, 183–86
American Bar Association 155
American Bar Association Formal Ethics Opinion 5
American Jurisprudence 127, 130–31
American Law Report Annotations 112, 146–47, 192–93
Appellate Court 44–48, 188–89, 202
Appellate Court decisions before 1935 are not binding 46
Appellate Defender 64–65, 214
Appellate Lawyers Association 65
Appellate Procedure Rules 149
Appellate Prosecutor 214
Appellate Review of Damages 55
Association of Legal Writing Directors (ALWD) 183
Attorney General 57, 95–97, 205
Attorney Registration and Disciplinary Commission 151, 154–55
Auditor General 214

Ballentine's Law Dictionary 145
Black's Law Dictionary 145
Bluebook Citation Manual xx, 181–83, 185–86
Board of Education 213
Board of Higher Education 213
Building Commission 216
Busharis, Barbara xviii, 160

Callaghan's Illinois Civil Practice Forms 132
Callaghan's Illinois Digest 66
Calleros, Charles 1
Capitol Fax 92
Cassette Tapes of Floor Debates in Illinois House 89
Chicago Bar Association 143, 155
Chicago Bar Association Professional Responsibility Committee 155
Chicago Bar Record 128, 142
Chicago Daily Law Bulletin 74
Chicago Journal of International Law 141
Chicago Law Times 141
Chicago Lawyer 65, 74
Chicago-Kent College of Law 140
Children and Family Services, Illinois Department of 206
Circuit Court of Cook County 202
Circuit Courts 48–55, 202–03

Citation of Legal Authorities 177–94
Citation Samples 187–93
Civil Procedure Rules 149
Client Interview Forms 163
Code of Illinois Rules 106
Code of Judicial Conduct 153
Collins, Maureen 182
Commerce and Economic Opportunity, Illinois Department of 207
Commerce Commission 212
Commercial Financing Forms 163
Compiled Statutes 78, 185, 189
Compiled Statutes Annotated 79, 150–52, 189
Comptroller 95, 206
Constitution (1818) 24–29
Constitution (1848) 29
Constitution (1870) 30–31
Constitution (1970) 31–33, 87, 187
Constitution, special citation rules 33–34
Constitutional Convention ("Con-Con") 18, 31
Cook County Forest Preserve 93
Cook County Jury Verdict Reporter 52
Corkery, John 135
Corpus Juris Secundum 127, 130–31
Corrections, Illinois Department of 207
Council on Developmental Disabilities 216
Court Clerk 121–22
Court of Claims 56–58, 100, 190
Court of Claims Reports 58
Courts Commission 153, 191
Courts Commission Reports 153
Courts, Administrative Office of Illinois 64

Crime Victims Compensation Act 57
Criminal Justice Information Authority 55–56, 215
Criminal Law Digest 64
Current Law Index 106

Department of Agriculture 206
Department of Children and Family Services 206
Department of Commerce and Economic Opportunity 207
Department of Corrections 207
Department of Employment Security 207
Department of Financial Institutions 208
Department of Human Rights 208
Department of Human Services 208
Department of Insurance 209
Department of Labor 210
Department of Natural Resources 210
Department of Nuclear Safety 210
Department of Professional Regulation 210–11
Department of Public Aid 211
Department of Public Health 211
Department of Revenue 211
Department of Transportation 211
Department of Veterans' Affairs 212
Department on Aging 206
DePaul University 140, 141–42
Descriptive Word Index 71
Developing confidence as a researcher 14
Dickerson, Darby 183
Digest Key Numbers available in Encyclopedias 134
Digests 66–72, 122–23
Diversity Jurisdiction 60–61

Index • 223

Domestic Relations Forms 163
Double billing of research time 5
Duggan, James 58, 86, 129, 132
DuPage County Bar Association 149

Educational Labor Relations Board 216
Electronic Forms 164
Electronic Legal Research 164, 195–216
Emergency Management Agency 208
Employment Security, Illinois Department of 207
Encyclopedias 127, 129–34
Environmental Protection Agency 208
Erie R.R. v. Tompkins 60
Estate Planning, Will Drafting, and Estate Administration Forms 163
Ethical duties of legal research 13–14
Ethics Inquiry Program 154

Federal Appendix 47
Federal Court Forms 164–65
Federal Question Jurisdiction 59–60
Federal Rules Decisions 151
Financial Institutions, Illinois Department of 208
Form Books 159–65

General Assembly 77, 89–92, 99–100, 196
Google 173
Governor 77, 78, 95, 205
Guardianship and Advocacy Commission 214

Haudenosaunee Great Law of Peace 20

Headnotes, never quote 66–67
Hein, Shannon 141
HeinOnline Law Reviews 141
Historic Preservation Agency 209
Honigsberg, Jan Peter 11
House Journal 89
Housing Development Authority 215
Human Rights Commission 215
Human Rights Reporter for Illinois 104
Human Rights, Illinois Department of 208
Human Services, Illinois Department of 208

Illinois Administrative Code 190
Illinois Appellate Court 44–48, 188–89, 202
Illinois Appellate Court decisions before 1935 are not binding 46
Illinois Appellate Defender 64–65, 214
Illinois Appellate Prosecutor 214
Illinois Attorney General 57, 95–97, 205
Illinois Attorney General 95–97
Illinois Auditor General 214
Illinois Bar Journal 128
Illinois Board of Education 213
Illinois Board of Higher Education 213
Illinois Building Commission 216
Illinois Causes of Action 163
Illinois Citation Rules 184–85
Illinois Civil Practice with Forms 132
Illinois Client Interview Forms 163
Illinois Code of Judicial Conduct 151, 153
Illinois Commerce Commission 212
Illinois Commercial Financing Forms 163

Illinois Compiled Statutes 78, 185, 189
Illinois Compiled Statutes Annotated 79, 150–52, 189
Illinois Compiled Statutes, State Bar Edition 189
Illinois Comptroller 95, 206
Illinois Constitution (1818) 24–29
Illinois Constitution (1848) 29
Illinois Constitution (1870) 30–31
Illinois Constitution (1970) 17–19, 31–33, 87, 187
Illinois Council on Developmental Disabilities 216
Illinois Court of Claims 56–58, 100, 190
Illinois Courts Commission 153, 191
Illinois Courts Commission Reports 153
Illinois Courts, Administrative Office of 64
Illinois Criminal Justice Information Authority 55–56, 215
Illinois Criminal Law Digest 64
Illinois Decisions 123
Illinois Department of Agriculture 206
Illinois Department of Children and Family Services 206
Illinois Department of Commerce and Economic Opportunity 207
Illinois Department of Corrections 207
Illinois Department of Employment Security 207
Illinois Department of Financial Institutions 208
Illinois Department of Human Rights 208
Illinois Department of Human Services 208
Illinois Department of Insurance 209
Illinois Department of Labor 210
Illinois Department of Natural Resources 210
Illinois Department of Nuclear Safety 210
Illinois Department of Professional Regulation 210–11
Illinois Department of Public Aid 211
Illinois Department of Public Health 211
Illinois Department of Revenue 211
Illinois Department of Transportation 211
Illinois Department of Veterans' Affairs 212
Illinois Department on Aging 206
Illinois Digest 66–72, 122–23
Illinois Domestic Relations Forms 163
Illinois Educational Labor Relations Board 216
Illinois Emergency Management Agency 208
Illinois Environmental Protection Agency 208
Illinois Estate Planning, Will Drafting, and Estate Administration Forms 163
Illinois Form Books 160–63
Illinois General Assembly 77, 89–92, 99–100, 196
Illinois Governor 77, 78, 95, 205
Illinois Guardianship and Advocacy Commission 214
Illinois Historic Preservation Agency 209
Illinois House Journal 89
Illinois Housing Development Authority 215

Illinois Human Rights Commission 215
Illinois Industrial Commission 215
Illinois Institute for Continuing Legal Education 99, 143
Illinois Jurisprudence 102, 132, 191
Illinois Jury Instructions 165–66
Illinois Jury Verdict Reporter 52
Illinois Labor Relations Board 169
Illinois Law and Practice 102, 132, 191
Illinois Law Finder 81, 126, 162–63
Illinois Law Office Practice Forms 163
Illinois Law Quarterly 141
Illinois Legislative History Guide 89
Illinois Legislative Service 190
Illinois Lieutenant Governor 95, 205
Illinois Liquor Control Commission 215
Illinois National Guardsman's Compensation Act 57
Illinois Office of Banks and Real Estate 213
Illinois Pollution Control Board 213
Illinois Prisoner Review Board 97
Illinois Property Tax Appeal Board 214
Illinois Public Employee Reporter 104, 169
Illinois Real Estate Forms 163
Illinois Register 98, 105, 107, 190
Illinois Revised Statutes 103, 185
Illinois Rules of Appellate Procedure 149
Illinois Rules of Civil Procedure 149
Illinois Rules of Professional Conduct 13, 149, 151, 153–54

Illinois Secretary of State 57, 95, 206
Illinois Senate Journal 89
Illinois State Archives 107–08
Illinois State Bar Association 64, 102, 143, 155
Illinois State Bar Association Ethics Opinions 155
Illinois State Board of Elections 212
Illinois State Police 209
Illinois State Treasurer 95, 97 206
Illinois Supreme Court 38–43, 188, 202
Illinois Supreme Court Rules 184–85, 189
Index to Legal Periodicals 106
Industrial Commission 215
Institute for Continuing Legal Education 99, 143
Institute for Paralegal Education 144
Insurance, Illinois Department of 209
Internet Searches 173–74
Iroquois Great Law of Peace 20

Jefferson, Thomas 22
John Marshall Law School 140, 142, 162, 172
Judicial Inquiry Board 216
Jurisprudence 102, 132, 191
Jury Instructions 165–66
Jury Verdict Reporters 52–55

Keefe, Thomas 172
KeyCite 120–21, 195
Kunz, Christina 171

Labor Relations Board 169
Labor, Illinois Department of 210
Law Office Practice Forms 163
Law Review Articles 138–43, 191–92

Laws of the State of Illinois 78
Leave to Appeal Table of Cases 121
Legal Citation 177–94
Legal Encyclopedias 127, 129–34
Legal Research Quiz 217–20
LegalTrac 141
Legislative History 82–89
Legislative History Guide 89
Legislative Reference Bureau 90
LexisNexis 4, 7, 58, 195–97
Library of Congress 196
Lieutenant Governor 95, 205
Liquor Control Commission 215
Local Court Rules 149
Local Ordinances 78, 93
Loislaw 4, 63–64
Looseleaf Services 169–75
Lorman Educational Services 144
Loyola University 140, 142

Maroon Book 183
McKnight, Jean 139
McMorrow, Mary Ann G. xv–xvi
Model Penal Code 146
Monroe, James 22, 25
Most Overlooked Research Resource in the Law Library 12

National Business Institute 143–44
National Guardsman's Compensation Act 57
National Jury Verdict Reporter 54
Natural Resources, Illinois Department of 210
Nichols Illinois Civil Practice with Forms 132
North Eastern Reporter 115–16, 185
Northern Illinois University 57, 140, 142
Northwest Ordinance 23
Northwestern University 140, 142

Nuclear Safety, Illinois Department of 210

Occupational Information Coordinating Committee 213
Ordinances 78, 93
Organizing research 10–12
Ottley, Bruce 135

Pendent Jurisdiction 60
Phillips, Joseph 25
Plagiarism 178–80
Polelle, Michael 135
Pollution Control Board 213
Posner, Richard 183
Practitioner's Handbook for Appeals 156
Professional Conduct Rules 13, 149, 153–54
Professional Regulation, Illinois Department of 210–11
Property Tax Appeal Board 214
Public Aid, Illinois Department of 211
Public Employee Reporter 104, 169
Public Health, Illinois Department of 211

Quiz 217–20

Real Estate Forms 163
Reference librarians 12
Removal of Actions to Federal Court 60
Reporter Services 170
Restatements 145–46, 192
Revenue, Illinois Department of 211
Rowe, Suzanne xviii, 160
Ruebner, Ralph 135
Rules of Appellate Procedure 149
Rules of Civil Procedure 149

Rules of Professional Conduct 13, 149, 153–54

Scalia, Antonin 77, 81, 83–86
Schanzle-Haskins, Ellen 58
Secretary of State 57, 95, 206
Senate Journal 89
Session Laws 78, 190
Shell bills 91
Shepard, Frank 112
Shepard's Daily Update Desk 118
Shepard's Federal Citations 116
Shepard's Illinois Citations 58, 93, 103, 105, 112–120, 153, 156, 166
Shepard's Law Review Citations 120, 128
Shepard's Northeastern Citations 115–16
Shepard's Professional and Judicial Conduct Citations 156
Shepard's United States Citations 116
Shepards on LexisNexis 114
Slavery in Illinois 26
Slip Opinions 63
Smith-Hurd Illinois Compiled Statutes Annotated 78, 150–52, 190
Sonderby, Max 52
Southern Illinois University 57, 58, 140, 142
Statutes from other jurisdictions 92
Sullivan's Judicial Profiles 73–74
Supreme Court 38–43, 188, 202
Supreme Court Rules 151, 184–85, 189
Suskin, Howard 144

Telephone as research tool 121–22
Textbooks 185
Teitig, Lisa Kuhlman xviii

Thomson Company 131
Transportation, Illinois Department of 211
Treatises 134–138, 191

Uniform Commercial Code 146
Uniform Laws Annotated 146
United States Bankruptcy Court for the Central District of Illinois 59, 201
United States Bankruptcy Court for the Northern District of Illinois 59, 201
United States Bankruptcy Court for the Southern District of Illinois 59, 201
United States Constitution 17, 187
United States Court of Appeals for the Federal Circuit 59, 201
United States Court of Appeals for the Seventh Circuit 59, 156, 187, 201
United States District Court for the Central District of Illinois 59, 187, 201
United States District Court for the Northern District of Illinois 59, 187, 201
United States District Court for the Southern District of Illinois 59, 187–88, 201
United States Supreme Court 187
University of Chicago 140, 142, 183
University of Illinois 57, 140

Vandalia 27–28
Veterans' Affairs, Illinois Department of 212

West's Illinois Digest 66–72
West's Smith–Hurd Illinois Compiled Statutes Annotated 78, 150–52, 190

Westlaw 4, 7, 58, 120–21, 195–97
Willard, Frances Elizabeth 30
Wojcik Secret for Using Digests 70
Words and Phrases 145

Wren, Christopher 48

Youck, David 64